Marriage Adventures overturns the notion that marriage has to become more stale the longer you're in it. This book is both inspiring and practical—a must-read for any couple that wants their first marriage to be their only marriage.

Ben Arment
Creator of Dream Year and STORY

Despite what our culture sometimes tells us, marriage is not an obligation to be dreaded. It's an adventure to be cherished. In this insightful book, Carrie and Erv show you the way.

Jeff Goins
Author, *Wrecked: When a Broken World Slams Into Your Comfortable Life*

Carrie and Erv have an inspiring, contagious passion about healthy marriages. In a time where marriage is bemoaned and lifetime faithfulness is rare, their rallying cry is one that needs to be heard—marriage can not only be good, it can be really fun.

Brandon Clements
Author, *Every Bush Is Burning*

A great marriage doesn't just come naturally, and thankfully there are resources like this book to encourage and teach us all how to be just a little bit better each day. Your marriage will be the better for reading it!

Bryan Allain
Author, *31 Days to Finding Your Blogging Mojo.*

Your greatest relationships in life are the result of shared adventure. Carrie and Erv wake up every morning and live life together as one great adventure. Their stories and practical wisdom inspire me to dream and live big.

John-Erik Moseler
Chief Adventure Officer, *The Wonder Grove*

Carrie has a unique way of sharing nuggets of wisdom in an engaging story-telling way. Marriage Adventures is thoroughly enjoyable, practical and full of timeless wisdom for couples at all stages of marriage.

Laura Krokos
Women's Development Coordinator, *Master Plan Ministry*

Carrie and Ervin have what every married couple wants. Their portrayal of their marriage and their brutal and humorous commentary on how they got it and nurture it will have you reading and re-reading this book. The family in America is suffering. We need more resources like this to change that.

Jonathan Pearson
Pastor, Blogger, Co-Director of *The Sticks* Conference

may your marriage be the adventure of a lifetime!

Carrie + Ervin

MARRIAGE ADVENTURES

The Secret to an Extraordinary Life Together

CARRIE & ERVIN STARR

DREAM YEAR

To Mikayla, Brianna, Connor and Karolin,

our favorite fellow adventurers.

CONTENTS

PART FOUR: THE TRAVELING JOURNEY

INTRODUCTION

Our marriage was doomed from the start.

Between the two of us, our parents have been married six times. The odds were stacked against us.

Fresh out of college, we believed our marriage could be different. We wanted our first marriage to be our only marriage.

We didn't just want our marriage to survive, we wanted it to thrive.

We wanted our marriage to be a great adventure!

For the past twenty years we have been brutally honest, financially savvy, and sleeping naked.

It has made all of the difference.

By living a bold life of adventure in our communication, our finances and our bedroom, most observers of our marriage think we are still on our honeymoon.

This book is our adventure story. From the moment we first met to our cross country honeymoon to our Alaskan anniversary, we share the secrets of our extraordinary life together with courage and transparency.

Hang on for the wild ride!

PART ONE

THE DATING JOURNEY

CHAPTER ONE

THE FRIENDSHIP FACTOR

Call me idealistic, but I always wanted to marry my best friend. This was tricky since my best friend in college was a short, strong-willed, redheaded female who made me crazy. Incidentally, she's now my sister-in-law and, besides my husband, is still my best friend.

I believe friendship is a strong foundation for any marriage. While marriage should certainly involve romance, ultimately a healthy marriage is a great friendship. Friends enjoy each other's company. They like being together. They look forward to seeing one another. There is a longing to simply be close to a good friend. Our daily activities and greatest adventures are best when shared with our friends.

Friends also communicate with each other. They go out of their way to tell you how they feel. Friends share ideas. They are honest with one another. They give each other good feedback. They tell you when you are screwing up big-time.

Best friends tolerate weaknesses in each other. They're not surprised when you aren't perfect. They know your flaws. True friends are patient and forgiving. They have to be, because there is no fooling them about who you really are. Best friends love you when you don't deserve it. Our best friends love us even when we let them down. They expect more from us. They push us to be better. A true friend looks for the good in you and finds effective ways to bring it out.

Every marriage needs this strong foundation of friendship. While passion levels rise and fall throughout a marriage, friendship keeps you bonded for life. When I was in high school and college, I longed for this kind of friendship in a spouse. While I loved my best friend Heather, I knew she would never be my life-long partner. The question remained: who would be?

When I first met Erv, I had no idea he would one day be my husband. As soon as I met him, however, I knew I wanted to be his friend.

At the first Campus Ambassadors Christian Fellowship meeting in the fall of my sophomore year of college, the crowd of students contained many new faces.

One in particular stood out to me.

He was short, wearing glasses, and sitting directly across the circle from me.

We each took turns sharing a story from our childhood. This guy decided to share two stories. And they were long stories… with lots of details… shared with enthusiasm.

I was intrigued.

When the meeting was over, I immediately walked across the room to introduce myself.

"Hi! I'm Carrie. I enjoyed your stories tonight. What was your name again?"

I remembered it being an old man's name, but it would not

stick in my head.

"It's Ervin. But you can call me Erv. Everyone does."

I couldn't decide which was worse, Erv or Ervin. Maybe he goes by a middle name, I thought, or another nickname.

Erv was a junior who had just recommitted his life to his Christian faith. After two years of living the typical college life, including a fraternity and an unhealthy dating relationship, he was looking for a fresh start. Making new friends and growing in his faith were top priorities for him.

Unfortunately, I was already running late for a resident advisors meeting so we weren't able to talk for long. I spent the next hour discussing floor activities and disciplinary procedures and when I returned to my dorm room, the girls on my floor bombarded me with questions. They said a short guy in a tie-dyed T-shirt had just stopped at every room on the floor looking for me. They all wanted to know who he was, but no one could remember his name. I didn't know what to tell them. I was not the kind of girl that guys came searching for.

It never occurred to me that the kid from Campus Ambassadors with the old man's name would walk clear across campus to see me.

The next day, as I sat in the back of my 11 a.m. class, I noticed someone in the front row. I couldn't tell for sure, but I thought it might be Erv. I leaned out into the aisle just a bit so I could see him a little better. It didn't help much. Having forgotten my glasses, the details were fuzzy. I would have to wait until the end of class to get a closer look. I spent the next hour distractedly planning how I'd see if it was him.

When the professor finally ended her in-depth analysis of Old Testament literature, I initiated my plan. I needed to get close enough to tell if it was really him without being too awkward if it wasn't. I had only met this guy once, so I wasn't entirely sure what he looked like. Did he wear glasses? I couldn't remember. This guy was wearing glasses.

As I neared the front of the room, I saw that he was talking to another friend of mine from the Campus Ambassadors group the night before. That settled it. It was definitely him. I re-introduced myself, and he said he remembered me. In fact, he had looked for me at my dorm the night before but couldn't find me anywhere.

Tie-dye guy mystery solved.

You never know when you're going to meet the person who changes your life forever. Even though I was curious about whom I would spend the rest of my life with, I wasn't really looking for him. I was busy enjoying my life. I loved being single. I valued my freedom and independence. I had dreams and goals and I was passionately pursuing them. I was confident in who I was and what I believed in.

These were the very characteristics that sent Erv looking for me after that initial meeting. He admired my confidence and strength. When we're living a full and vibrant life, I believe we are the most attractive to others.

After re-discovering each other in class, Erv and I decided to have lunch together. We enjoyed getting to know one another better over the high-calorie cafeteria food. It was amazing how easy it was to talk to someone I had met just the night before.

We ran into my friend Rachel on our way out of the dining hall. I introduced her to Erv and then he said his goodbyes. As soon as he was out of sight, she gave me the third degree.

"Who is that guy? How do you know him? Is he the one who

was looking for you last night? I heard about that. Do you like him? You guys would make a perfect couple. You're the same height. And you have the same skin tone."

I didn't realize that matching height and skin tone made the perfect couple. Apparently this was a winning combination. I explained that I had just met him and had too little information to determine if I "liked" him.

That night, as I was procrastinating instead of doing my homework, my phone rang.

It was tie-dye guy.

"Are you going to breakfast?" he asked.

"Probably not," I replied.

I usually had a piece of fruit or a granola bar on my way to class, allowing me to sleep as late as possible yet not starve.

"Well, John and I are going to breakfast at seven, and we want you to come too."

"Um ... sure. Sounds like fun."

I was really thinking, "Sounds pretty early." But, it was nice to be invited, and I didn't want to say, "No."

Half asleep and slouched in the semi-comfortable chairs of the dining hall lobby, John and Erv were waiting for me the next morning at 7 a.m. I was amused at their lethargy when it was their idea we meet at this hour. We dragged ourselves up the stairs and ordered our breakfasts. The dining hall was deserted so we had our choice of seats.

Once we sat down and started talking, all three of us were wide awake. We found ourselves in the midst of a passionate debate. I don't remember the exact topic of conversation, but it was obvious all three of us had strong opinions. Though it was tense at times, we enjoyed ourselves and respected each other.

We decided we should do this again. Soon, we became "The Breakfast Club," meeting twice a week to share, talk, argue, and pray. This was the birthplace of our refreshingly honest friendship.

Erv and I found ourselves spending more and more time together. In addition to breakfast and lunch, we added dinner to our joint schedules. I moved up to the front row by Erv in our "Bible as Literature" class, and we met in the park or the library to do our homework together. We went to Campus Ambassadors meetings on Thursday nights, and he helped lead my small group Bible study every Tuesday night. Between classes, meals, Campus Ambassadors, and church, we were seeing each other almost every day. Erv quickly became one of my closest friends.

Through our friendship, we discovered there are many fun adventures to be had for little to no money. When we hear the word adventure, we often think of exciting escapades that take us to far off places and come with a high price tag. One of the most rewarding parts of adventure is the creativity involved. You don't need to journey outside your own backyard to enjoy a thrilling quest. Erv's ability to make every day experiences an adventure was one of the qualities I first admired in him. Other than the limited income we earned from our work-study jobs on campus, we were both broke in college. Finding creative ways to have inexpensive fun became a favorite pastime of ours.

ERV'S TAKE

For most of us, our entertainment expenses expand to the size of our income. As we earn more, we find more costly forms of entertainment. Our culture encourages this "upgrading." Here are a few simple examples:

We used to rent movies ($1-$3) and watch them at home. Now we might go out to a movie at the theater ($20-$30) depending on if we get snacks—and that's just for the two of us. If we take the whole family of five to the movies it can be $40-$60. In either case, we simply watched a movie.

We used to go for dessert or coffee ($2-$10) and now we can afford dinner and dessert ($25-$75).

We used to play catch at the park, but now we might choose to go golfing with friends or instead of sled riding we might go skiing (big cost differences with similar fun and time together).

We have to stop and ask ourselves a few important questions:

1. **How much are we willing to spend on fun and entertainment?**
   The more we spend on fun and entertainment, the less we have for other things (a home, cars, giving, etc.).

2. **What kind of memories and family culture do we want to create?**
   For us, we want time together to be a high priority and we want our family to have

a sense of adventure. We also want to be generous with others and live the reality that fun does not always mean spending lots of money. This creates better balance for us than simply looking at what we are "able" to spend now.

3. **Is it worth going into debt?**
   Since we believe debt is a form of bondage, we don't take on debt, ever, for our adventurous life. We would rather save for a costly opportunity (like a trip) or opt for less costly opportunities (like a hike in a state park) than take on debt.

Early in your marriage, you may have very little money for fun outings. I would encourage you to let that be a time for learning to be creative (cook a new meal together at home). Enjoy the simple and free (hike a nearby natural wonder). Learn to avoid the enslaving power of debt (keep to what is affordable today). Dream about tomorrow (you can save and enjoy imagining what the real experience will be like in the future). Consider the kind of family memories and culture you want to create.

Having fun is one good use of money, but over-spending will only feel fun for a short time. Later, it will feel horrible. It is a bit like an all-you-can-eat buffet. After over-indulging in all your favorite foods, you end up with a bellyache.

Our early friendship was based on enjoying lots of free fun. When you're focused on friendship rather than romance, you spend less time pretending. A lot of romantic relationships begin with trying to impress each other. We put on an act and find ourselves saying and doing whatever we think the other person will enjoy. This is a dangerous trap. Eventually, the relationship progresses and you're discovered for who you really are. The act is not sustainable and the connection fails.

Friendship doesn't put on an act. Otherwise, it's not true friendship. Friendship allows you to be yourself. You can take risks and be honest about your feelings and opinions. Your shared experiences are built on genuinely common interests that you can enjoy for a lifetime.

From the beginning of our relationship, Erv and I learned to be real with each other. Our faults and flaws were on display as well as our passions and favorite past times. By the end of just one semester of friendship, it seemed everyone on campus was talking about "us."

The interrogation by Rachel after that first lunch back in September was just the beginning. If I had a dollar for every time someone asked me, "What was going on?" between Erv and me, I could have given up my tutoring job at the campus learning center and bought a new car... or at least a new bicycle. Every girl on my floor was convinced that Erv liked me, and they kept pushing me to talk to him about it.

Meanwhile, I was trying to be content with our friendship and not hope for something more. Finding a friend like Erv was a rare gift and I didn't want to ruin it.

Erv was pretty sick of the comments as well. He had his share of friends tell him he should be dating me, but he would always blow them off. There was a girl or two back home that he liked, and he wasn't even sure if he was staying at our college. He was thinking about transferring as soon as the following semester. He was happy to have a good friend in me and that was it.

End of story.

Fortunately, that's not the end of the story.

CHAPTER TWO

RELATIONSHIP INVOLVES RISK

Rejection is one of the worst experiences imaginable. We hide in the safety of familiarity to avoid rejection. There are so many opportunities we would love to pursue, but we don't for fear of failure. We cling to safety. If we only knew what we were missing by staying safe, we would take so many more risks.

I grew up playing it safe. I was taught to plan and consider the possible negative outcomes. Risky situations were to be avoided. "You can't be too careful," was my mantra.

By the time I arrived at college, however, I was sick of playing it safe. I didn't want to be reckless or careless, but I did want to take some risks and try things I'd never considered doing before—things like jumping off a bridge!

Each September, our Campus Ambassadors group would take a canoe trip down the Sacandaga River. On that trip during my freshman year, there were a couple of local teens jumping off a bridge as we pulled our canoes out of the water.

It looked like a blast to me, but no one else from our group wanted to try it. We got in our cars and drove back to campus. I now had a new goal—next year I was going to jump off that bridge!

The next year's canoe trip was just weeks after Erv and I met. We spent three hours as canoe partners—chatting, singing, and cracking each other up. We pulled our canoes out of the water and I excitedly headed for the bridge. No one wanted to go with me.

When I climbed to the top of the bridge, Erv got all serious. "You're really going to jump off that? How do you know it's safe?"

"I saw a bunch of people do it last year. It'll be fine."

"Do you know how deep it is?" Erv inquired.

"Nope. I'm sure it's fine," I yelled from the top of the bridge.

"You're crazy. I'm gonna check it first." Erv waded into the water and swam down to the bottom, far below me.

When he popped up out of the water he said, "Seems like it's at least ten to twelve feet deep. You're about 30 feet up there. You should be okay."

"So are you coming?" I asked, sitting with my feet dangling over the edge.

There was a long pause. Erv slowly made his way out of the water and up to the top of the bridge beside me. "You sure you want to do this?" he asked.

"Yep!" I stood up.

Erv eventually stood beside me. "On three…"

We both counted loudly to three and jumped! As my feet left the bridge, I felt a strong sense of irreversibility. We hung in the air for what felt like an eternity. I kept waiting and waiting for my feet to hit the water. Together we made an incredible splash!

As we swam to shore, others from our group started climbing the bridge. Some jumped. Others turned back in fear. Erv and I celebrated! We had taken a risk and it was worth it.

Taking risks is scary.

When we share how we honestly feel about someone, it is one of the greatest risks of all time. Our minds race considering the possibilities. What if the other person doesn't feel the same way? What if they want nothing to do with us anymore? What if there is no turning back and we ruin our friendship forever?

Romantic relationships never start without a degree of risk.

After being hassled by my girlfriends for months, I allowed myself to take a risk and initiate a "define the relationship" conversation with Erv. I sat nervously on his dorm room floor while he sat on his bed, caught completely off guard by the topic. He wasted no time making it clear that he didn't have any romantic feelings for me. In fact, he told me point blank, "I will never date you, so you can get that idea out of your head."

He was pretty clear. I put the idea out of my head. Or at least I tried to.

Most of us have a list of the qualities we are looking for in a partner. There are particular physical attributes and personality characteristics that we find attractive. We may not have a written list, but in our heads, the list is there.

Erv had a list. While I lived up to many of his hopes and expectations, there were other areas where I fell short.

Most problematic, he didn't find me attractive. No big deal, right? Wrong. Fortunately, Erv now says he's not sure how that was ever possible.

He also wanted to be with someone athletic. While I am active and adventurous, let's just say I'm not the most coordinated girl you've ever met.

While Erv didn't see me as romantically compatible with him for these reasons, we somehow managed to maintain our close friendship.

When choosing a life partner, we all look for someone we find compatible; someone who matches us. We rule out a lot of possibilities for this reason. This could mean a missed opportunity. We'd be better served to find a good companion. A true companion has some of the same interests and goals as you but they are not necessarily similar to you in personality and temperament.

In addition to not being a cover model and sucking at sports, there are other reasons why Erv and I were not compatible.

I like to stay up late. He likes to go to bed early.

Erv loves to start projects. As soon as he gets them up and running, he's on to the next big idea. I love to plow through a project and see it through until it's complete. I am an obsessive finisher.

I enjoy being surrounded by lots of people. Erv thrives on his alone time.

While the differences are challenging, companionship wins out over compatibility. Because we were such good companions, we stayed in touch over the long Christmas break. Erv decided not to transfer and I was relieved, not wanting to give up my new friend. I didn't allow the rejection of Erv not having romantic feelings for me to ruin our friendship.

Rejection does not need to leave us devastated. Sometimes, it makes us stronger.

We both made visits to each other's houses over the holidays and enjoyed getting to know our respective families. Seeing where we both came from continued to strengthen our friendship. We were surprised to learn how many similarities there were in our backgrounds.

We'd both grown up in broken homes and lived with single parents. Our houses were modest and our family cars were in need of repair. Yet because of our parents' economic struggles, we'd both been brought up with the values of hard work and careful financial planning.

These shared principles have been critical to the success of our relationship. Instead of feeling awkward, we were right at home as we sat on each other's hand–me-down furniture, eating homemade cookies while playing cards with our parents. We didn't mind waiting to use the one bathroom because we'd both grown up with only one in our homes. And we both dressed in layers because the heat was turned down at his house and at mine. Nothing about our home lives needed to be apologized for or explained. We each enjoyed having a friend who considered the other "normal."

While sharing the same background is certainly not required for relational success, appreciating and understanding the other person's upbringing is crucial to your marriage. The way you were raised will make an impact on your future family, whether you intend it to or not.

As we spent time with each other's families, we were reminded of our parents' generosity while growing up. I shared with Erv that when my mom received some unexpected cash, she used it to buy groceries and secretly left them for a struggling friend at the nearby trailer park. Erv shared that his mom used to bag up her kids' outgrown clothes and share them with the less fortunate family next door. In high school, my mom allowed a friend of mine to live in our home for months while her parents' house was under construction. Erv's home was always open to friends and family members who needed a place to stay.

As we continued to trade stories back and forth, it was obvious our parents were characterized by helping others in need. Hearing these stories helped us appreciate our common roots of giving regardless of income. Since we attended church together regularly, I noticed Erv was committed to giving weekly. At first this surprised me since he was always short on cash. I learned he was committed to give this money, even if it was a small amount. He also supported a child in Haiti through Compassion International each month. I admired this generosity and appreciated his understanding of my own convictions regarding giving. For me, donating a portion of my income at church was a joy. Helping young women through the support of a Christian rehabilitation home was also a priority to me.

Though some of our friends didn't understand how we could have "extra" money to give away when we didn't have money for CDs or pizza, it was something we respected and admired in each other. It was yet another value we held in common.

ERV'S TAKE

When it comes to generosity, it is never too early to start. Many of us think, "When I have more, then I'll be able to help." You are developing habits and patterns now. Be generous now.

What you have to give—money, talent, time, friendship—is valuable. Your decision to give consistently and generously will make it part of who you are, building itself into the fabric of your family.

Don't wait to bless others. Today is the day you are sure to have and today is the day God wants to use you to make this world better for someone else.

When you see the world around you as being one of abundance rather than one of scarcity and limitations, you are free to be more generous. It is a strange reality that God has woven into our world. When we sacrifice something for another person, we end up feeling really good about that generous act. We were built to bless one another through our generosity.

This also means we should be quick to accept the generosity of others.

Sometimes we cannot see the truth right in front of us. We need other people to speak into our lives and help us make wise choices. When we're young adults, it's easy to neglect the advice of others. It can be especially tempting to ignore the advice of our parents.

After years of living under their direction and guidance, as young adults we often resist our parents' wisdom. We want to prove we can make decisions on our own; that we're all grown up and no longer need their help.

This is foolishness on our part. We have truly matured when we can hear and appreciate our parents' advice. In the spring of my sophomore year, my mother gave Erv and me some advice that would change our relationship forever.

Erv was soon heading home for the summer. I was staying in town to work with the church youth group. We had become the best of friends in every way, and we were already plotting how we'd stay in touch across the miles. In the last weeks of classes, we decided to have a movie marathon night and watch all three installments of *The Godfather* with our friend John. Our good buddy John got tired during the first movie and left us alone in my dorm room for the next six hours.

This was a mistake.

I have a high sensitivity to violence, and *The Godfather* movies are full of people being kicked, punched, and shot. Every time someone pulled out a gun or beat someone up, I would cringe and go into hiding. As this process repeated itself over and over again, I found myself sitting closer and closer to Erv. When the last movie ended I realized we were uncomfortably close and in the room all alone. After the whole, "I'll never date you," comment though, I figured we were safe.

That's when he kissed me.

I no longer believe anything he says.

The next day Erv apologized for kissing me and asked if we could pretend it didn't happen. I was disappointed but agreed. We didn't want to mess up our perfect friendship.

That night he kissed me again.

Throughout that week we had many long, awkward conversations about our relationship.

Here's what I didn't know at the time. A few weeks earlier, Erv was visiting me at my dorm room. I don't remember this at all, but I guess I bent over to get something out of my closet. Erv caught himself checking me out!

At first, he told himself, "Gross, that's Carrie!" as if I was his sister. That's when he realized maybe I was more attractive than he thought. At least from behind!

Erv had been praying for God to give him feelings for me if He wanted us to be together. This was an interesting answer to prayer.

Apparently, he wasn't the only one who started to find me attractive either. Erv had finally convinced the other guys in our Christian fellowship group that he wasn't interested in me. Now more and more guys starting hanging around me. They were just friends as far as I was concerned, but a degree of jealousy made Erv look at me differently.

He knew if I started dating someone else, our unique friendship would change significantly and he didn't want that to happen. Maybe he had romantic feelings for me after all.

Then the kiss happened. And the next one.

By then, the romantic feelings were very much alive.

We came to the mutual conclusion that we were interested in being more than friends, but we feared ruining our friendship. We'd both dated other people before and had our hearts broken. Neither of us was interested in signing up for more heartbreak, and we didn't want to risk hurting each other.

We didn't know how to proceed, except Erv wanted to keep kissing me, which I told him had to stop. If he wanted to kiss me, he had to date me. Don't you admire my high standards?

We decided we needed a little outside help with this one. We made an appointment with our campus minister, who was a trusted friend and father figure to both of us. He told us there was no way to enter a relationship without risk. We couldn't guarantee where our relationship would go. He explained that moving from friendship to romance was part of God's plan for creating families. Did we consider each other someone we would want to marry someday? We both thought that was a possibility.

He then gave us some warnings and guidelines regarding our physical relationship if we were to start dating and agreed to pray with us about our relationship.

Then we had an unexpected conversation with my mom. She called me at my dorm room when Erv happened to be there. I gave her an update on what was going on between us right there in front of Erv.

I told you we were really open and honest with each other.

When I was finished, my mom asked to speak with Erv. I nervously handed over the phone. She shared with him about her own tragic love story.

She had been abandoned by my dad before I was even born. When I was in middle school she became good friends with a man named Al. They played board games together, had long talks, and enjoyed each other's company.

Over time, they fell in love, and Al asked my mother to marry him. My mom said "no" because she didn't want to disrupt the lives of my brother and me. We'd never had a father, and she didn't think it was fair to ask us to accept him as our dad.

Al was disappointed but understood. He gave my mom space and moved on. I remember being sad because I really liked Al… maybe even loved him.

Years later when I went off to college, Al came back. Now with my brother and me all grown up and on our own, he wanted to know if my mom had room in her life for him again. They began dating and started planning a future together.

At the beginning of my sophomore year of college, Al got very sick. He suffered from depression during the years that he and my mom were separated, and he didn't take very good care of himself. He didn't see the doctor, and important medical issues went unaddressed. By the time he was reunited with my mom, the damage to his heart had been too great.

He died during my first week of college that year, the very same week I met Erv.

His passing was a great loss to my mother. She couldn't help but regret postponing her future with Al.

She told Erv on the phone that night that there are no guarantees of the future. She said that if we loved each other, we needed to act now and enjoy one another while we could. She ended her conversation by telling him to "Go for it!" because today was the only day we had for certain.

That night we officially started dating.

Thanks, Mom.

CHAPTER THREE

CHILDLIKE BEHAVIOR ENCOURAGED

Most people take themselves way too seriously. We're all fallible. We're going to make mistakes. We'll try something, fail, and look pretty stupid along the way.

So what? When you get over your fear of looking dumb, you begin to really enjoy your life.

You take risks, accept challenges, overcome obstacles, and achieve what you considered impossible. It's an incredible experience to live without fear of what others think. There is no place where this principle is more evident than in a romantic relationship.

Love makes people stupid. When you first fall in love with someone, you act all kinds of crazy. That's part of the fun!

If you take yourself or your relationship too seriously, no one enjoys themselves. I've met way too many couples where one person or the other overanalyzes everything they say and do in their relationship. They are tortured about the potential of messing up their perfect connection.

Being in a healthy relationship should make you feel more

secure about who you are and what you do, not less. Stop thinking so much about your relationship and just enjoy yourself— even if it means making mistakes and looking dumb.

This is a lesson I learned very early on in our relationship. Erv and I officially started dating when the spring semester was almost over. We were just days away from spending three long months apart for summer vacation. Our timing was terrible.

We had one Saturday left to spend together, and we wanted to make it special. I had been telling Erv about a nearby state park I thought he'd love. It had a beautiful lake with a nice beach and great hiking trails. We packed an elaborate picnic of peanut butter and jelly sandwiches along with snacks confiscated from the dining hall and headed out mid-morning.

We became a little nervous, seeing the clouds get thicker and darker while driving to the park. By the time we arrived at the beach, we found ourselves in an absolute downpour. We sat in the car trying to wait it out, but it was clear that this storm was here to stay.

Fighting off our disappointment, we decided to somehow salvage our last special day together. We climbed into the back of the borrowed 1984 Bronco and set up our picnic.

I grabbed an apple in one hand and a banana in the other and started singing, "I like to eat, I like to eat, I like to eat, eat apples and bananas."

I was surprised when Erv joined in on the next verse and started singing, "A lake tae ate, I lake tae ate, I lake tae ate, ate, apples and bananaise!"

This song is so silly, and I was delighted Erv was willing to sing it with me! As the rain got louder on the roof of the car, our singing got louder. Soon we were screaming the song at the top of our lungs. "O loke to ote, O loke to ote, O loke to ote, ote opples ond bononos!"

I'm sure we looked and sounded absolutely ridiculous. I loved it! As the song ended, we both cracked up laughing at ourselves. We then proceeded to sing more silly camp songs for the next two hours until the sun finally reappeared.

Looking stupid in front of each other has never been an issue for us. If anything, acting ridiculous has become an assumed expectation. We are both committed to absurd childlike behavior.

A lot can be learned from acting like children. Kids thoroughly enjoy themselves without being overly concerned about what others think. Our relationships are richer when we allow ourselves to behave like kids. Children make the most of every moment. They are creative and see more than the difficult circumstances at hand. Kids see the possibilities and find ways to navigate around challenges.

Have you ever noticed that children are also quick to forgive your mistakes? They don't hold grudges or punish you when you mess up. They want to restore the relationship so they can get back to the fun. While some childlike behavior could be considered irresponsible or inconsiderate, in general, our relationships are stronger when we choose to be like kids.

Kids are also pretty open with their feelings. They don't beat around the bush or try and hide things. If they like you, you'll know it. If they don't, you'll know that too. Being vulnerable and sharing your feelings honestly is critical to a strong relationship. Your communication will be so much healthier if you express your childlike heart.

Our first summer as a dating couple, we became expert communicators across the miles. In 1991, we were unaware that the

Internet had even been invented, so email was not an option. We didn't have cell phones either. We both became proficient at writing old-fashioned letters.

I lived in an apartment with some friends for the summer, and I quickly learned exactly what time the mailman arrived each day. In fact, there were many days when I would meet him at the mailbox. We became good friends.

After talking almost daily for an entire school year, it definitely took some time to get used to being apart. The letters were a wonderful opportunity to put into words the new emotions and ideas we were both experiencing. We nurtured our honesty and openness through writing.

The time apart also forced us to grow as individuals and pursue our separate interests. This was a healthy change for both of us as our lives had become so intertwined. It's essential to continue growing as individuals if you want your relationship as a couple to thrive and be healthy.

About once a week we would catch up over the phone. We enjoyed hearing about the other's adventures and discoveries. That summer we also enjoyed occasional in-person visits, which were a big deal. I appreciated getting to know his "at home" friends better, and he would tag along at my youth group events. We both gained newfound gratitude for one another's talents and abilities.

We counted down the days until we were back together at school. Erv moved into an apartment off-campus with John and some other friends. I moved back on campus and resumed my resident advisor duties.

Since many of our friends hadn't seen us since May, they didn't know we had started dating. Last year, we had finally convinced everyone that there was nothing going on between us—and now there was. This was going to be complicated.

In many ways, growing our relationship off the radar of others was a huge advantage. We've seen so many dating couples suffer because of the intrusion of well-meaning friends.

Sometimes, it can be helpful to get advice about your relationships from close friends and family. No one knows you better. However, most unsolicited advice is a nuisance.

The most damaging feedback I've seen is when outsiders push you into a more serious relationship faster than you're ready. This phenomenon seems especially common when two friends begin dating. Apparently everyone has been waiting for you to finally realize you're perfect for one another and now that you have, people suddenly have you walking down the aisle. When others are in a hurry to push your relationship to permanent, it puts way too much pressure on both of you.

Sometimes you simply need to ignore the feedback from others. If it gets obnoxious, you may need to have an honest talk about how their meddling is impacting your relationship.

It's also challenging when friends start treating you differently just because you're dating. We were afraid this would happen to us when the new semester started up. The first time we showed up at an event holding hands, everyone stared. It was a little like being in junior high school.

We were so glad when the demands of classes started to increase and everyone finally had homework to do. We were tired of our relationship being the center of people's attention.

After we got past all of the annoying, "I told you so!" comments, people almost started acting normal around us. Fortunately, no one was pressuring us to get married anytime soon.

There were other challenges to our newfound status of "dating."

The word "dating" seems to imply going out somewhere and spending money. In fact, some would argue that in a committed dating relationship this should happen on a fairly regular basis.

Being separated over the summer had saved us a lot of money. Our major expenses were postage and the occasional long distance phone call. Now that we were together in person, we were curious how we'd fit going on dates into our budget.

The "spending money" we both had accumulated barely covered school-related expenses such as textbooks and testing fees. There wasn't much leftover to be spent frivolously. We would need to enjoy one another's company in ways that were creative and, more importantly, cheap. Fortunately, our common love for the outdoors kept a world of inexpensive opportunities open to us.

ERV'S TAKE:

While it is true we show love to someone by spending money on them and giving them costly gifts, it is also true that we show love through time, creative effort, kind words, and good decisions.

I encourage you to date. We have been doing so for over 20 years and don't intend to stop anytime soon. But, love each other enough to make good decisions about how much to spend on dating. You can enjoy one another's company and communicate how much you value each other without spending a lot of money.

Research on happiness indicates that we derive more long-term joy from multiple, smaller pleasures than from a single, more expensive pleasure. For example, if you get $2,400 in gift money for your wedding, you could take a trip to Disney World (a good deal of fun that lasts a week – and creates life-long memories) or you could do 24 $100 dates (one each month for the next 2 years) – which will also create lots of memories and give you two years of enjoyable experiences.

Our favorite date destination became the local park. Town parks are a fabulous free option for year-round outdoor fun. Whether you enjoy sports, reading, wandering, or daydreaming, you can enjoy hours of pleasure together with no price tag. There were two wonderful parks in our small college town, allowing us a little variety.

My favorite place to escape was Wilber Park. Not only did it have a great playground and picnic area, it had walking trails meandering through the woods. I enjoyed this park almost weekly during my first two years of college. Before meeting Erv, I would venture to the park after a long day of classes. I'd wander through the woods listening to my Walkman, forgetting about homework, roommates, and tests.

I enjoyed bringing Erv to this special place. We'd pack our picnic lunches from the dining hall and enjoy them in the shade of the huge walnut trees. Then we'd hit the trails together and talk about whatever happened to be on our minds that day. Sometimes we'd tell stories from our childhood. Other days we'd share our dreams for the future. I continued to be intrigued by Erv's openness and valued his honesty, even when we disagreed.

Erv's favorite park was Neawah. This was where the Oneonta Yankees played baseball, and many of their games were free to college students. We enjoyed cheering on the home team while munching on hot dogs and drinking from our water bottles that we filled with tap water.

Neawah Park also had great open fields for playing Frisbee or tossing a football. Growing up without a dad, I'd never played catch in the yard like the other kids in my neighborhood. This was a favorite childhood pastime of Erv's, and he was anxious to share it with me. Neawah Park became my sports training camp where I tried my best to keep Erv's boyhood hobby alive. It was a test of his patience and my humility—good lessons for both of us.

The playground at both parks is where we could be the most childlike. We designed elaborate obstacle courses, challenging ourselves to use as many pieces of the equipment as possible. We were especially pleased when we crafted a route where our feet never touched the ground.

After we had the passage planned out, we would time each other making our way across the monkey bars and suspension bridges. If the other person's time beat our own, we'd have to make the course more complicated.

I'm sure our competitiveness provided some great entertainment for onlookers at the park. Sometimes the local kids would end up joining us in our little competition. It was on one of these occasions that I saw a different side of Erv.

A small boy, who seemed about four-years-old, slipped off the monkey bars and landed hard on the wood chips below. Before I was fully aware of what had happened, Erv was bent over checking this small stranger for bumps and bruises. He treated the boy with such tenderness and compassion. He dried the little guys' tears with his shirt sleeve and safely returned him to his mommy.

In that moment, I got a glimpse of the man I wanted to be my husband. I had thought it before, but this time, I could see it. It was scary and exciting all at the same time.

As the beauty of fall gave way to the chill of winter, we stayed committed to our dates in the park. Bundling up in layers, our boots would crunch along the snow covered paths of Wilber Park. Sometimes we'd build snowmen in the picnic areas or dodge snowballs while running across the fields. The frozen pond at Neawah was open for free skating, and we'd chase each other in circles around the slippery ice.

Our most childlike winter endeavor was when we retrieved some cardboard boxes out of the recycling room in my dorm. We fashioned them into sleds and proudly took them to the park. Admiring their speed, the neighborhood kids asked to take turns with our cardboard creations. We set new records in our homemade sleds.

Another fabulous free date is a trip to the library. While it may not sound like the most romantic location, libraries are magical. There are so many wonderful worlds to be discovered through books. New skills can be learned, ideas acquired, and resources revealed. Some libraries offer the most beautiful settings to enjoy a good book together. Find a quiet corner, hidden loft, or a secret stairway. If you don't want to spend a lot of time at the library, you can take out a book and share it in a setting you enjoy more.

When you read, as a couple or individually, you always have something new to talk about. Learning together allows you to grow together, which then deepens and strengthens your relationship. Reading together was a central part of our dating experience. It remains one of our favorite shared past times today.

We would select a book from the library and then take turns reading chapters aloud to each other. Sometimes we'd take our book to the park and other times we'd just sit in the living room at Erv's apartment. We enjoyed discussing the characters and guessing where the plotline was headed next. We were challenged with new ideas about education, business, theology, and leadership.

We also continued to be study buddies and helped each other with our homework. Erv was my math expert, and I was his typist.

It was a good arrangement.

Enjoying these simple childhood pleasures established our relationship on a great foundation of carefree fun. By ignoring social pressures and unsolicited advice, we found ourselves plunged into a world of whimsy and delight—a place we've refused to leave for the past twenty years.

CHAPTER FOUR

THE GIFT OF CREATIVITY

Showing love to others can be tricky. Some of us are really comfortable expressing our feelings. Others find this to be a tough challenge. To have a successful relationship, you'll need to improve your ability to communicate love. Fortunately, this is easy to do when you study how you've been uniquely made.

Each of us has a way we more naturally express ourselves. The way you communicate love may not be the way others around you show their love. When we compare ourselves to them, we can feel pretty incompetent. When we believe we're bad at showing our feelings, it can stop us from even trying.

The first step in learning to effectively communicate love is to stop comparing yourself to others. My friend Krista is fantastic at showing love through serving. She is always making meals for folks, watching other people's children, making late-night pickups at the airport, etc. She blesses me with these wonderful acts of service all of the time.

Sometimes I feel terrible about it. I'm pretty sure she outserves me at least two to one. When I compare myself to her, I feel like a lousy friend. While I do enjoy showing love through practical acts of service, it is not my most natural way to communicate love.

I am a words girl. I adore words and use about 7,000 of them every day. I want my words to communicate love and appreciation for others around me. In fact, my personal mission statement is, "to make the love of God tangible to every person I meet." I do this primarily with my words. Whether it is the students in my classroom, the clerk at the grocery store, or my teenage kids, I try to show love and appreciation for every person I meet throughout the day.

Fortunately, my serving friend Krista feels blessed by my words. We meet once a week to walk and talk. I love listening to her stories and encouraging her. This is the gift I enjoy giving the most. It's also a wonderful gift to me as she listens to my thoughts and shares her words with me. We both feel loved by our quality time together.

Spending extended time together like this has always been a natural way for Erv and I to show love to one another. We both enjoy long, lingering conversations where one subject runs endlessly into another. This is how our relationship first started. All those long talks in the park or over dinner where we'd completely lose track of time formed a strong bond between us.

Maybe you're better at showing love through serving than you are at using your words. Perhaps your gift of love is the extended time that you're willing to offer in your busy schedule. Maybe you're better at expressing yourself through gifts.

Some people are really good at giving gifts. They are extremely thoughtful. They pay attention to the little details about you. They know what color you like to wear, the kind of music you listen to, your hobbies and interests. They take great care in choosing the perfect gift.

My mother-in-law is excellent at this. She is a very thoughtful gift giver. I don't quite know how she does it, but she always knows exactly what to get for me. Part of what makes her gifts so precious is the obvious time and effort she puts into selecting the gift. When she gives, she is giving part of her heart.

When Erv and I were first dating, one of the ways we wanted to show love to each other was through gifts. Once you have a significant other, it's almost expected to give gifts for birthdays, holidays, etc. This doesn't have to be a burden. Gift giving can be a fun way to explore your creativity. Some of my favorite presents of all time are creative, outside-the-box ideas.

As the florist was delivering rose bouquets to girls on my floor in college, Erv was out picking wildflowers by the side of the road. For special occasions, we exchanged our share of greeting cards made from construction paper and magic markers. We also both tried our hand at writing poetry. At the time, our poems seemed very romantic and meaningful. Reading them now is just plain embarrassing!

Imagination and resourcefulness can serve you well when it comes to gift giving. Erv and I both had the desire to show love and appreciation to our families at Christmastime. Instead of buying overpriced gifts we couldn't afford, we decided to make them. We copied poems and favorite Scripture verses onto ordinary printer paper. Next we very carefully burnt the edges of them attempting to give them a charred aged look. We completely torched a few, but overall we were quite successful.

We placed the ones we didn't incinerate into dollar store frames and wrapped them in comics from the Sunday paper. This was the wrapping paper of our childhood. They actually turned out beautifully and everyone loved them.

Probably the most favored of all our homemade Christmas presents were the coupon books entitling our loved ones to household chores, a listening ear, or a big bear hug. We gave these to our parents, siblings, friends, and roommates. Our parents appreciated the household chores when we were home, and our roommates enjoyed making it our turn to clean the toilet! Though we made these in college, Erv's mom recently redeemed one of those coupons for a night out with her son. That gift lasted much longer than anything we could have bought at the mall.

As Erv's 21st birthday approached, I wanted to do something really special for him. A homemade card or second-rate poem was not going to do. I could think of countless things to buy, but an expensive gift was out of the question. I decided to use all the resources at my disposal and plan an exceptional experience instead.

Creating a unique experience can be even more meaningful and memorable than a physical gift. With a little ingenuity and some extra effort, it's also a less expensive way to express love.

Waking up at 6 a.m., I grabbed my guitar and walked the two miles between my dorm on campus and Erv's apartment downtown. I woke him up by throwing rocks at his bedroom window. The sports training at Neawah Park was coming in handy! I attempted to serenade him from the driveway below and then offered him a breakfast of chocolate croissants that I'd picked up at the nearby bakery.

While he was at class later that day, I took tissue paper and streamers and wrapped his car like a giant present. When Erv finally got through the wrapping, his car was filled with balloons and an invitation to dinner. When he arrived at the designated location, I had filled our friend's apartment with tea-light candles and prepared him a delicious homemade meal.

This remains one of Erv's favorite birthday memories (though I still try to top it every year). I enjoyed planning it, executing it, and paying for it. I saved a lot of money by not purchasing an expensive gift and we had a fantastic day together.

The concept of saving money for the future eludes most of us. This fascinates me because we all have dreams for the future; dreams that will cost us money: a wedding, home ownership, vacations, retirement. Unfortunately, we won't accomplish any of these dreams without having a plan for saving.

Saving is a challenge because it requires having extra money to put away. Who has extra money lying around waiting to go into a piggy bank?! When we have money, most of us spend it. All of it, and then some.

We charge our expenses on credit cards. We take out loans. We spend every dime we have and then we spend more money we don't have. Savings seems impossible. When we were in college, Erv proved to me that savings is possible, even when you're broke.

ERV'S TAKE:

We have encouraged many couples to start where they are when it comes to savings. It may be as little as $5 or $10 a week to start. Save anyway – even when it is just a small amount. Your first goal should be an emergency fund of $500 to $1000. Celebrate each milestone along the way (e.g. each time you save another $100).   By celebrate I mean smile, shout, dance, high five, a joyful kiss...you get the picture.

If there is something you really want like a piece of furniture, trip, musical instrument, or piece of technology (e.g. a new couch, a guitar, a new iPad) you can save the money a little at a time. It becomes a goal – you learn amazing life lessons. You learn about waiting, patience, diligence, delayed gratification, and the sense of achievement. You also will discover what things are most important to you: you might start saving for one desire and along the way determine something else is more important (and you'll be so glad you didn't spend the money!).

After dating for about a year, we found ourselves talking about "The Future." I was unaware of this at the time, but as talk of marriage became a reality, Erv literally began saving his pennies to purchase an engagement ring.

I found out later that he was intentionally breaking bills to make more change. He'd go home and put the change into a huge glass jar that he kept hidden in his bedroom closet. When it wasn't adding up fast enough, Erv started saving his one dollar bills as well.

After being diligent for the entire year, my intelligent boyfriend started researching quality rings at discount prices. He was determined to pay cash and wanted to get the best ring he could, at a price he could afford.

This system of saving change for a future big purchase has

been employed by the Starr family for two decades now. Not only is this how Erv purchased my engagement ring, and his first guitar, it's also how we save for our family vacations. The whole family is motivated to fill up the jar so we can get away together. The savings jar plan is proof that small amounts of money, saved up consistently over time, can add up to a big reward.

While Erv was busy saving for my ring, another school year came to an end. He was graduating, and I was preparing for my senior year. When I moved off-campus into an apartment for the summer, I couldn't find my class ring. It wasn't in the box with my other jewelry. I assumed it had been misplaced while rushing to get packed.

In the meantime, Erv went on an unexpected trip out of town. I honestly don't remember the excuse he gave me, but with my ring missing, I was a little suspicious. Stealing my ring would have been the perfect way to ensure buying the properly sized engagement ring.

That summer, Erv and I worked together with the church youth group. To make sure we were appropriate examples to the teens, the church leadership asked us to refrain from acting like a couple around the students. We didn't hold hands or hug or any other "couple-like" things. It was actually fun for us to pretend there was nothing going on between us for a whole summer. We enjoyed the kids we worked with and had a great time being a team. It was a wonderful opportunity to learn how our different strengths as leaders worked together.

By the end of the summer, there were several parents telling us that we would make a great couple. We tried not to laugh out loud at them.

As the summer came to an end, I was getting ready to begin

student teaching. My birthday was coming up, and Erv wanted me to go camping in Maine with his family to celebrate. I was torn because my co-operating teacher invited me to help her spend the week before school setting up her classroom. This was a good opportunity for me, and I really felt obligated to do it.

Erv was insistent that I find a way to go with him. I couldn't help thinking about the missing ring last May and wondered if this was why Erv was being so adamant. I didn't want to miss out on what could be a most memorable engagement birthday, so I worked out a compromise. I would help out at the school for most of the week and then enjoy a long weekend camping.

Erv's entire family greeted me when I arrived the day before my birthday. We spent the afternoon enjoying Old Orchard Beach and then the giant water slide at the campground with his younger brothers and sister. I helped his mom and grandmother cook dinner that evening, and later we sat around the campfire playing cards. Erv and I made plans to get up early to watch the sunrise the next morning for my birthday.

I was nervous and excited. It sounded like a perfect proposal opportunity, but I didn't want to be disappointed. I made myself believe that nothing was going to happen and tried to get some sleep.

The next morning Erv's mom hurriedly woke us up. Apparently whatever alarm we'd set didn't go off, and the sky was already beginning to brighten. Frazzled, we quickly jumped into the car. We drove down to the beach and parked in a one-hour tow-away zone. Erv grabbed a brown paper bag and his guitar. I snatched the blanket packed by Erv's mom, and we ran down to the water's edge.

As we spread out the blanket, the sun was just starting to

come up over the horizon.

Our timing was perfect after all.

We sat together quietly enjoying the beautiful red and gold of the sunlight contrasted against the dark blue sky. It was gorgeous.

Several minutes passed before Erv finally broke the silence. "Do you want your birthday present?"

By now, I was so nervous, I could barely speak. This was rare for me. I nodded my head.

He handed me the brown paper bag. I opened it and tried not to act disappointed. It was *The Prophet* by Frank Peretti. It was a book we'd wanted to read for awhile. I'd been excited about it all summer until that moment.

This was not the special present I was hoping for.

"Thanks," I said, trying to be sincere. "We can start reading it today."

I hugged the book to my chest and stared out at the ocean. Maybe I should have just stayed back and helped out more at the school. Maybe things weren't going where I thought they were going. I was a fool to get my hopes up.

That's when Erv pulled the guitar out of its case.

He started singing a song I had never heard before. As he sang, I realized that it was a song he had written.

He sang about our friendship and the many things he valued about me. It was overwhelming. I went from feeling awfully disappointed to feeling very loved and appreciated.

Then I heard a line in the song I couldn't quite make out. The waves were crashing and the wind was blowing, but I thought I heard him say, "… and I ask you if you'll marry me?"

It couldn't be what he just said. I didn't want to assume it and be wrong…again. How many times could I be disappointed in one morning?

Then the song ended. Erv put the guitar aside and got down on one knee.

This time the message was clear. "Will you marry me?" he asked.

I was so nervous; I didn't know what to say.

Of course the obvious answer is, "Yes!" It would have been the right answer. It's what I wanted to say. But it's not what came out of my mouth.

I have this terrible habit of making jokes when I'm nervous. Humor is supposed to relieve tension and awkwardness.

Even though I was hoping and even somewhat expecting this to happen, I found myself completely unprepared for the awkwardness of the moment. "I'll think about it," was the humorous reply that came out of my mouth.

Erv fell over in the sand.

I was not funny.

I quickly regained my senses and told him, "Yes, of course!" as I helped him up out of the sand.

Being gracious, he forgave my nervous humor. He pulled the simply beautiful quarter-carat diamond ring out of his pocket and placed it on my finger.

Wait until the youth group parents hear about this!

CHAPTER FIVE

PATIENCE AND SELF-CONTROL

For two decades we've been working with young adults. The majority of them imagine themselves married someday. Many of them hope to be engaged before they graduate from college, especially the girls. Marriage is definitely an exciting adventure to look forward to, but it's a journey, not a destination.

When we spend more time dreaming of getting married instead of developing our own skills, interests, and pursuits, we're likely to be disappointed when we achieve our "married" status. A successful marriage requires two whole, growing people. The more satisfied and engaged you are with your individual life, the more energy and emotional health you have to bring to your marriage. If you're looking for another person to complete your life, you'll find marriage disappointing.

We were like many of the college students we've worked with over the years. Once we were finally engaged, we were anxious to be married. As we began looking at our academic calendars, spring break seemed like a perfect time for our wedding. I had a week off from college and Erv had a week off from the seminary he was attending. We set our date for April 3rd and began making preparations.

Our parents, who had been very happy for us up until this point, were not pleased with the date. They thought it was too soon. They wanted us to wait until August so I could focus on student teaching and finish my degree before getting married. We found ourselves in the midst of a conflict.

Despite the tension it caused, Erv and I decided to tentatively move forward with our April plans. We were grown-ups, and it was time to start making decisions on our own. Hopefully our parents would come around and see it our way.

As we counted down the days, other issues came to the surface. Now that we were getting married, the temptation of physical intimacy became stronger. We both had a commitment to sexual purity before marriage and had struggled to maintain our mutually agreed upon boundaries while dating. Being engaged only made it more difficult to exercise self-control. After failing to respect our boundaries on multiple occasions, we recognized what we considered to be a serious problem. If we couldn't trust each other to have self-control before we were married, how could we be sure we would honor one another and be faithful to each other after we were married?

We decided we needed to maintain absolute purity for a significant amount of time before we could call each other "husband" and "wife." If we could not, our relationship could not move forward. We've seen this same pattern in countless young couples we counsel. Maintaining sexual purity before marriage is a struggle for most dating and engaged couples. We have a natural desire to mirror the closeness of our emotional relationship in our physical relationship.

It's a pretty natural and swiftly moving process.

We've seen incredible rewards come from waiting. By exercising self-control before marriage, both partners are assured of their spouse's ability to say "no" to temptation. It also allows you to focus on showing your love for one another in different ways. You see your communication improve as well as your ability to show respect and honor to each other. These are important skills for your marriage.

By sticking to your convictions, you also prevent a pattern of having guilt be associated with sex. When couples violate their physical boundaries while dating, they start a cycle of intimacy followed by regret, ending in blame. They often struggle to undo this pattern and can't fully enjoy their sexual relationship once they're married. We counsel dating and engaged couples not to rob from the pleasure of their future sex life. When it's protected as a precious treasure for the future, sex is more fully enjoyed later as a married couple.

This doesn't mean waiting is easy. It's not. At least it wasn't for us. Physical touch and closeness is a primary way of expressing love for both of us. Now that we're married, this is a huge advantage! Before we were married, it spelled danger on a regular basis.

We needed to unlearn some unhealthy habits if we were going to keep our commitment to purity. One habit we needed to break was spending the night at each other's place. Back when I was a resident advisor, I had my own room with two beds. Erv's dorm was on the complete opposite side of campus from mine. After many late night conversations, game nights, and even prayer meetings, it was easy to let Erv crash in my room on the other bed.

At first I worried that this looked bad. I lived in the only all-girls dorm on campus so a guy leaving in the morning was pretty obvious. After a few months of this happening almost once a week, we went from looking bad to actually being bad. Why would Erv sleep in that other bed when we could stay in the same one and fall asleep in one another's arms?

This is when we discovered the phenomena of "horizontal permission." There is an unspoken permission given when we're in love and horizontal together. We're more comfortable, vulnerable, and willing to try things we wouldn't otherwise if we were on our feet, or even sitting upright. A half-sleepy, horizontal state is a bad position from which to make good decisions and exercise self-control.

We not only needed to stop having sleepovers, we needed to stop all mutual horizontalness. Naps, massages, wrestling, and all other combinations of potentially horizontal behavior were temporarily eliminated from our relationship. We were serious about our commitment to honor our boundaries and went to extreme measures to stay within them.

Fortunately, now that I lived off-campus, I had a roommate. And she was pregnant. That was double protection against fooling around at my place. Erv was also living off campus now and lived in a one-bedroom apartment with two friends from seminary. Our friend John had the only bedroom and Erv and Rob stayed on beds set up in the living room. Since we had zero privacy, we were extremely safe there as well.

We also had my pregnant roommate and Erv's seminary buddies holding us accountable. If we left town for one of our many road trips, our friends would call and ask how it was going.

We never stayed alone together but arranged to crash at places where we could sleep in separate rooms (and sometimes, separate tents). We didn't want to let our friends or each other down.

It was at this time that we reconsidered the wisdom of our parents and changed our wedding date to August. Not only did their preferred, later date give us the time of purity we felt was essential, it also allowed us to employ many cost-cutting strategies for the wedding.

The new date allowed plenty of time to make our own invitations, favors, decorations, and gifts for the wedding party. The extended time also made it possible for us to explore more options for reception halls, photographers, and DJs. As a result, we found an inexpensive fire hall for the reception, I learned that the husband of one of my college classmates was a photographer who was willing to give us a great rate, and Erv's second cousin offered to be our DJ at a significant discount. These discoveries did not come quickly but rather were the result of careful research over time.

In addition to the money saved, an August wedding date meant we could take an extended honeymoon. Erv was now a full-time graduate student in seminary. The program was rigorous and ran 11 months of the year. He had short breaks at Christmas and Easter, but he was off the entire month of August. Since I would be finished with college and awaiting a full-time teaching job to begin in September, we realized we would be free to take a one-month honeymoon!

With all of these benefits, we wondered why we hadn't listened to our parents' advice sooner. In this one decision we had honored our parents, established greater trust between each other, saved money, and quadrupled the length of our honeymoon.

This was delayed gratification at its best!

The fall semester passed quickly. Student teaching was rewarding but challenging. I didn't have a vehicle so I had to carpool with a fellow student teacher working in the same building. Most days one of us would need to go in early or stay after late. By the middle of the fall semester, I was leaving for school before dawn and coming home in the dark every day. Sharing a ride did, however, allow both of us to save significantly on gas for the 60 mile round-trip drive each day. Every dime of that savings went into our wedding fund, along with all of Erv's spare change.

Meanwhile, Erv's graduate work buried him in the study of Hebrew, Greek, and theology. The seminary he attended was located out-of-state so he had to travel on a weekly basis for classes. He too found carpooling to be an economical solution as he shared a ride with three other seminary students from across New York State. Every week he and his friends would drive six hours to the seminary, sleep on the floor of a local church to avoid paying hotel costs, attend eight hours of classes, and then drive the six hours home. This not only saved him money, but he developed some great relationships with the other guys in the car. The remaining five days a week were spent reading textbooks, writing papers, fulfilling learning contracts, and volunteering 20 hours a week in ministry. Erv definitely felt the increase in difficulty as he moved from undergraduate to graduate level work.

Once we had busier schedules, it added new challenges to our relationship. Our free time was limited so we had to be creative as we looked for ways to spend time together. We were both renting apartments now, and fortunately, we lived only two blocks away from each other. This allowed for spontaneous opportunities to cook dinner for each other or at least stop in for a brief work break. Erv would drop off Elmer's glue to help me with a project I was making or I would walk over just to tell him "goodnight." We would leave encouraging notes on each other's front doors. These served as reminders that even though we didn't see each other much, we were thinking of each other. I decided to volunteer in the same ministry as Erv so we could see each other at least one evening a week. He occasionally drove me to school just so we could talk in the car. We were glad this situation was temporary and looked forward to one day living under the same roof.

ERV'S TAKE

All over the world, most people find ways to sacrifice and stay within their financial means, even when that means riding a bicycle, sleeping on the ground, or limiting themselves to two simple meals a day. Our sacrifices seem simple in light of all we've seen in our travels to needy parts of the world, and they were worth it. For most of us, there will always be things we want but can't afford. They would make life easier, or so we think. The truth is that when we sacrifice, we gain a sense of trust in God's ability to meet our needs. We experience and bring out the generosity of others. We learn contentment with what we have and gain appreciation for the new things we gain.

When it comes to your wedding, it's a special day

worthy of some extra expenses. It's also just one day on what you want to be a lifelong journey together. Start that journey right. Spend what you can afford. The memories will be rich no matter the cost. For the honeymoon, I'd give the same advice. Enjoy each other and make special memories together right from the start. And begin now to be the couple you want to be—one who avoids spending what you don't have to do things you don't need.

Already married? Remember to be a blessing to the new couples in your life. Celebrate with them. Coach and encourage them toward wise decisions. We know how much work a great marriage is when it's forged in the shared experiences of triumph and challenge.

CHAPTER SIX
SIMPLY WED

Planning a wedding is quite an adventure. You have one special day to mark the beginning of the rest of your lives together. You want to get everything right. Many girls spend years dreaming about this day. Some have a collection of bridal magazines hidden under their bed. Others have a "Someday..." wedding board on Pinterest. We girls collect images of all the perfect elements to make our special day complete. We assemble and arrange them, practicing for the day when we can put our plans into action.

I had plans of my own before I met Erv. I wanted an outdoor wedding with lots of wildflowers and whimsy. I wanted my reception to be an awesome party with loud music and dancing. I didn't want a stuffy, formal affair. Now I finally had my chance to make it all happen.

I didn't realize how stressful it would be. When you plan a wedding, there are many expectations to manage. Obviously those of your future spouse are most important, but you also have the opinions of your parents and future in-laws. The pressure to please others and yourself can be challenging.

Planning your wedding can also be a wonderful opportunity to express who you are and who you want to be as a couple. While the input from others can be helpful, be sure to stick to your priorities. Honor the preferences of family when you can, but be sure you end up with a day you can enjoy and treasure.

We knew we wanted a big, fun, yet simple wedding. We also knew we were committed to paying cash and were unwilling to go into debt. In some ways, this made the myriad of decisions we had to make easier. There were many options that simply weren't available to us. Since we didn't have the money, it was easy to say "no" to many possibilities.

Unfortunately, many couples will go into debt to have their dream wedding. This one single day will cost them money for years and years to come. Add the interest to those debt payments and the total cost is overwhelming.

While your wedding day is certainly a most important day, it is not more important than your marriage. Starting your married life with unnecessary debt is a burden you don't need. Save where you can on your wedding so you can invest more into the rest of your life as a married couple.

As we planned our simply beautiful wedding, we found the biggest expense to be providing food at the reception. This was going to be a problem. We had a guest list of more than 300 people that neither of us was willing to cut in order to reduce our costs. Our friends and family were a high priority, and we didn't want any of the special people in our lives missing this important day. There must be a creative way to accommodate a large number of people. A very unconventional idea came to me.

"Have you ever been to a pot-luck dinner?" I asked Erv.

"Yeah. Our family does them all the time," he said.

"Okay great! Why couldn't we do that for our reception?"

"Do you think it would really work?" he asked me.

"I think it'd be perfect!" I answered.

"Sounds good to me." Erv said. "You take care of the details and just tell me when and where to show up. I'll be planning the honeymoon."

I was getting pretty used to hearing this line. I began to wonder why I even asked his opinion.

I was so excited about this idea, I got right to work. Because we were renting a fire hall, we were welcome to bring our own food. This was a huge advantage over other reception locations that required you to use their catering service. Erv's large extended family graciously offered to cook extra food to ensure there'd be enough for out of town guests. Erv's aunt volunteered to make our wedding cake as her gift to us. Both of our moms started picking up extra bottles of soda every time they went to the grocery store, and I began stocking up on paper products.

As the invitations went out requesting people bring a dish to pass, we received many encouraging comments about how weddings used to be done like this "back in the day." Our guests were enthusiastic about our reception reminiscent of days gone by. We were excited to know we could accommodate the 230 guests that replied "yes!" to our invitations.

This out-of-the box idea got us thinking about other typical wedding expenses. Since all of my bridesmaids were poor college students and struggling recent graduates, we decided to buy material and sew the bridesmaids' dresses ourselves. My friend Meg spent countless hours creating the finished products.

As I looked at options for my own dress, the price tags made my head spin. Though I was hesitant, we pulled my mother's wedding dress out of her back-room closet. It was a perfect fit! And it was so much prettier than I remembered from the pictures I had seen growing up. After a trip to the dry cleaners, the dress was like new. I now had a beautiful wedding gown that meant so much more —and cost so much less—than anything I could have bought at the store.

It wasn't easy accepting help from so many people. As young adults getting married, you want to make your own mark on the world. There's a temptation to prove you can provide for yourself. We've seen so many couples stubbornly say "no" when friends or family try to provide assistance.

If help comes with strings attached, it may be wise to say "no." You don't want to be manipulated into changing your priorities simply because someone else is paying the bill. If you receive support from others, it should be in alignment with your own preferences. If not, you're better off providing for yourself or seeking assistance elsewhere.

Manipulation and guilt from outside your relationship put unnecessary pressure on your new marriage. Establishing healthy boundaries and guidelines during your engagement and wedding preparation will benefit your marriage relationship for years to come.

When help is given freely without expectations, don't be too proud to accept it. Your wedding truly is a community event. The more friends and family you involve, the richer the experience will be. Don't be afraid to ask for help and have enough humility to accept it.

Also be sure to express genuine appreciation for those who assist you. Because we were married in the nineties, I made mixed tapes as thank you gifts. I enjoyed choosing songs and personalizing each one to fit each individual. While I couldn't give a gift of money, I gave the gift of my time.

ERV'S TAKE

10 Tips to Keep Wedding Costs Reasonable:

1. Invite friends and family to use their gifts (musicians, photographers, florists, bakers, designers). These shared talents make great gifts and add a personal touch to the wedding.

2. Consider your venue: A firehouse might be too low class for you, but you can choose a place that doesn't require catering.

3. DIY: You can create centerpieces with wildflowers, devise beautiful lighting with candles or create ambiance with Christmas lights.

4. Consider a consignment shop for a dress: Have it altered to fit you well, but you can find amazing wedding dresses that have been worn once.

5. Consider the time of day: You can keep costs lower if you use a church or banquet hall on

a lower use day (Monday - Thursday. Even Friday or Sunday is cheaper than Saturday). You also impact the cost of food. Lunch is less costly than dinner and finger foods and dessert even less costly. A simple cake and coffee reception is a fine alternative.

6. Consider a pot-luck meal: This might not be for everyone, but it worked well for us. I have a large family who has many great cooks and a tradition of large gatherings. Every-one brings a dish to pass and the selection is amazing.

7. Natural Beauty 1: You could get married outside at a friend or family member's home or at a picturesque public park.

8. Natural Beauty 2: Skip the salon and make a memory having family and the wedding party help each other get ready for the big day.

9. Technology: Unlike 1993 (when we got married), novices are now able to take in-credible photos, make quality video, and de-velop extensive play lists with the technolo-gy right in their own pockets.

10. Keep the wedding small: Okay, truth is, I hate this one, but for some of you an inti-

mate wedding with your closest friends and family are exactly perfect. Disclaimer – I am in no way advocating excluding everyone or a Vegas wedding with an Elvis look alike! Simplicity is the key to a magical, affordable wedding.

While I was busy with wedding details, Erv was—true to his word—planning the honeymoon. We both love camping and traveling, so we decided we would spend our first month of marriage on a cross-country road trip. What a perfect way to start this incredible adventure together!

Growing up on the east coast, neither of us had spent much time down south or out west. Erv crafted a route taking us through as many states and national parks as possible during our four-week time frame. We followed the southern route out and the northern route back. Our landmark destination would be the Grand Canyon, a place we'd both always dreamed of going. With Erv's 1984 Ford Tempo in need of serious repair, Erv's grandparents offered to loan us their more reliable Subaru to increase the odds of us making the trip safely.

We started making an inventory of our camping supplies for the big adventure and realized we were missing many key items for our cross-country survival. Fortunately, we made this discovery as we were registering for shower and wedding gifts.

As friends and family members ventured out shopping, they did not find china patterns or sterling silver on our gift registry. They were surprised to find camp stoves, lanterns, sleeping bags, and coolers instead. We knew we wanted camping to be part of the Starr family lifestyle, and these items would serve us better than fancy dishes reserved for special occasions. This also allowed us to save significantly on our honeymoon since these supplies ensured we would not need to pay for hotels or restaurants on our cross-country trek.

I think bridal registries are one of the greatest gifts on earth. Be practical and think about what you'll need for the next several years when you register. Visit the homes of friends who have been married for a year or two and ask them what they use the most? What can they not live without? You'll get some great ideas you may not have thought of before.

Be sure to include items at a variety of price levels. Some folks will not be able to spend as much while others can be more extravagant. It's thoughtful to provide lots of options for people.

While it's good to be practical, remember these are gifts. It's okay to have some frivolous and fun items on your gift registry. I always look for these items when I'm headed to a bridal shower or wedding. If you've got games, toys, books, or something funky to decorate with on your list, I'm going to buy it for you!

Even with a gift registry, you may receive multiples of the same item. Here are a few options to consider. If there are selections on your list that you were super excited about and you didn't receive them, take back the multiples and buy what you really want. This option is a lot of fun! In fact, I would carefully consider the return policy when choosing where to to register. Choose a place that allows store credit without a receipt. Not everyone is good about getting a gift receipt. I know I'm not!

If you have storage space, you may want to keep your multiples for the future. I'm not sure why, but we received lots and lots of bath towels and glasses. Fortunately, we were encouraged by others to keep them. Once you start a family, you can never have too many towels. And once one glass breaks, it seems like they all do. Or, maybe we are just clumsy. At any rate, we went years and years without needing to buy towels or glasses. It was great shopping for free in our storage closet!

A third option for those multiple gifts is to re-gift them. I know this is a controversial subject. If you feel badly about giving a gift previously given to you, stick to options one and two described above. However, if you're in a stage of life where you're broke and you've been invited to several weddings in a row; it may be a great option for you. This was us for a long, long time! If the item is new and your friends would enjoy it, feel free to give it. My only caution is to make sure you keep track of who gave you what. This is essential! You wouldn't want to re-gift something back to the original giver. If it's a shower gift, make sure the giver is not in attendance. That's really embarrassing. Yes, I know from experience.

As our wedding day drew closer, we were humbled at the amount of help we continued to receive making this upcoming event a reality. The list of people we needed to thank on our ceremony programs got longer and longer. One friend offered to video the wedding and reception. Another set of friends wrote a song they would perform at the ceremony. My girlfriends helped me make centerpieces, my future sister-in-law made favors, and another friend helped turn all of our pictures into slides for a slide show at the reception. Both of our families threw us bridal showers, and our friends hosted a third shower in our college town. It was humbling to be on the receiving end of so much generosity.

The night before the wedding, our friends and family continued to bless us with their hard work and helpfulness. We spent hours at the fire hall blowing up balloons, hanging streamers, and setting up tables. We had decided against an outdoor wedding in case of rain. It was cheaper to rent the fire hall than a tent with tables and chairs. It was still going to be a fantastic party!

As we set the chafing dishes out on the empty food tables, we were humbled at the thought of our 230 guests providing our wedding feast. Once the reception hall preparations were finally complete, we attended our rehearsal and rehearsal dinner. In addition to all the food they were preparing for the coming day, Erv's family also cooked all of the food for our rehearsal dinner. With a wedding party of 16 people, it was a generous gift. When the food was gone, it was time for the guys and girls to go their separate ways. I said goodnight to my fiancé for the last time.

I wondered what marriage would be like. Since my parents were separated before I was born, I never experienced marriage in my daily life. I had visited the homes of friends and family members who were married. I knew how marriage appeared on TV and in movies. Some of these examples were inspiring while others were absolutely frightening.

Erv and I had been through weeks of pre-marital counseling. We were told the odds were stacked against us. My father had been divorced twice. Erv's mother had been divorced twice. The marital blueprint we'd both inherited was severely flawed. We would need to rewrite a new pattern of marriage for ourselves. We would need to demonstrate levels of patience and forgiveness we'd never experienced in our homes.

I could not have taken this step if it were not for my faith in

God. I knew I lacked the strength to unconditionally love someone for the rest of my life. As I looked forward to marrying Erv,
I knew I could not put my hope in him either. My hope for our
future marriage needed to be in someone bigger than both of us.
Without Christ, I lacked the courage to make a commitment.

We both agreed that divorce would not be an option for us.
We wanted our first marriage to be our only marriage. We were
going to start a new generation where we kept our promises and
followed through on our commitments. We would not abandon
each other or our future children. We dared to be different.

It was 2 a.m., and I couldn't sleep. I was excited and nervous.
I tossed and turned for hours. By 5am I gave up on sleeping.
I headed outside and went for a walk. The sun slowly started
to light up the early morning sky. It's finally here, I thought.
Our wedding day begins. With my friends still sound asleep, I
grabbed a blanket and spread it out on the lawn. I laid in the early morning sunshine for at least an hour, thinking, praying, and
reading my Bible. It was already warm on this first day of August. The sky was clear and beautiful. Today was going to change
everything. I soaked in my last few moments of complete independence and solitude, then slowly gathered my things and
headed toward my future.

My friends and I spent the morning picking purple Heather
and Queen Anne's Lace in the fields near Erv's grandparents'
house. We arranged them in mason jars and decorated the church
and reception hall with our homemade bouquets. Erv and his
friends busied themselves painting directional signs and posting
them along the country roads so none of our guests would be
lost on their way to the ceremony. Though it was tempting to
both of us, we avoided seeing each other as we criss-crossed our

way around the small town with our last minute errands.

The church had a small, detached building across the parking lot serving as a meeting hall. We planned on this spot being my dressing room. My bridesmaids showed up in their beautiful flowered dresses, while I arrived in my red plaid bathrobe. I delayed putting on Mom's wedding gown, not wanting the fragile fabric to get wrinkled or stained.

We snuck around to the back door to avoid being seen by the guests. It was locked. My mom checked the front door. It was locked too. Confusion erupted among the wedding party as we all tried to determine who had the key. As the minutes ticked by and the key was yet undiscovered, I became more anxious. As the hour of our wedding grew closer and closer, the parking lot grew busier and busier. I did not want to march through a crowd of arriving guests in my bathrobe to change in the church rest room.

It was now five minutes before 3 p.m. and I was desperate. I do not like being late. I certainly didn't want to be late for my own wedding. As we stood in the backyard of the church meeting hall, I surveyed the landscape. Taking inventory of the distance to the nearest road, the few houses facing the yard, and the tall trees scattered around the perimeter, I determined my current spot of grass would serve well enough as my changing room.

I wished for a bush or some shrubs to hide behind, but there weren't any. We decided to create a human barrier instead. I had my bridesmaids, my mother, my aunt, and a cousin circle up around me as I dropped my bathrobe and struggled to quickly slip the wedding gown over my head. Since everyone I knew in the world was out of view in the parking lot or seated in the church for my wedding, I comforted myself with the thought that if anyone had seen me, I had only exposed myself to complete strangers. Just as my mom was pulling up the zipper, our pastor came around the corner with the missing key.

Now that I was fully dressed and looked like a bride instead of a hospital patient, we all scurried across the parking lot just in time for the mothers to be seated. I had almost caught my breath by the time Canon in D started playing. It was my turn to walk down the aisle.

As my brother and I stepped through the double doors, I was overwhelmed at the crowd that stood before me. The church was full of all the special people I had known throughout my lifetime. While we slowly made our way down the aisle, I looked into the eyes of so many people I loved. These were individuals who had supported me, encouraged me, and cared for me as I had grown from a little girl into a young woman.

Then, as I looked straight ahead, I met the eyes of the man who would soon promise to support, encourage, and care for me the rest of my life. No man had ever kept such a promise to me before. I could hardly believe it was possible, but I filled myself with hope that it was true. This was the moment I had been waiting for.

As we approached the altar, I took Erv's hand. Our pastor prayed and then shared about the meaning and commitment of marriage. He challenged us to remember that marriage would require more from us than any relationship ever had in the past. We would need to be willing to serve, sacrifice, and forgive each other on a daily basis and it would take incredible resolve to make it work.

We had heard this before in our pre-marital counseling. In

fact, our pastor had told us in one of our sessions that most people would not get married if they knew in advance how much work it would really be. He believed the fact that "love is blind" was actually a great blessing keeping us moving forward toward the impossible.

When our pastor ended his sermon on the joys and challenges of marriage, he then transitioned into the sharing of vows. He looked first at Erv and asked, "Will you take this woman to be your wedded wife; to love and to cherish, in sickness and in health, for better or for worse, until death do you part?"

Honestly, I was nervous about this part. I wasn't entirely sure how to answer this question. Since you're asked, "Will you …?" the grammatically correct response would be, "I will." However, when you watch movies or TV shows, the bride and groom usually say, "I do."

Because I tend to over-think things, I had gone back and forth about which I would say. I was thankful that Erv was going first. I decided to say whatever he said so we would match.

Apparently, Erv had given his response some thought as well. As the pastor finished his question, Erv responded in a loud, clear voice for all two hundred and thirty guests to hear, "I most definitely do!"

I was completely surprised by Erv's enthusiastic response. I was also at a loss as to what I would say on my turn. I certainly couldn't respond the same way as Erv. His response was perfect. It was a classy move that made me feel treasured. How could I simply say "I do" or "I will" after that?

I tried to think of something quickly. As demonstrated by my completely inappropriate response to Erv's perfect marriage proposal, I am not charming under pressure. This was my wedding day. Words are my specialty. Surely I could come up with wonderful words expressing my love and devotion.

The pastor then looked at me and asked, "Will you take this man to be your wedded husband; to love and to cherish, in sickness and in health, for better or for worse, until death do you part?"

I responded, "Absolutely!"

It was the best I could come up with under pressure.

Charming as we both sounded, neither of us had a clue what we were saying.

PART TWO

THE NEWLYWED JOURNEY

CHAPTER SEVEN
GREAT EXPECTATIONS

Ah, the honeymoon. You've been counting down the days to this blissful getaway for two. All of your hopes and expectations will soon be fulfilled. It's a wonderful time to look forward to. It can also cause some anxiety.

Most men I know would be happy to skip the whole wedding process and jump straight to the honeymoon! Erv made this offer on more than one occasion during our engagement. There were stressful wedding planning moments when I agreed this would be a lovely option.

Most women, and even some men, are a bit anxious about the actual wedding night. Whether you've had sex before or not, there are high hopes for a perfectly romantic evening.

Don't expect perfection the first time around. Lower your expectations and just enjoy yourself. Once you're married, you'll have plenty of opportunities to get it just right. Great sex takes practice. The mechanics seem obvious, but it's the subtle details that make sex really incredible. Discovering exactly what your spouse enjoys is part of the fun. Learning to please your spouse is not a one-night mission but rather a life-long journey.

Our honeymoon got off to a rocky start. Here is a wonderful yet terrible truth about your own wedding: everyone you know and love in the whole world is there, in one place, at the same time. For a social girl like me, this was incredible! I was having an awesome time with all my friends and family at the reception. Erv literally had to drag me off the dance floor when it was time to go. We had our first married argument in the gaudily decorated getaway car because I wasn't quite ready to leave the party.

Fortunately, by the time we arrived at the charming 1860 farmhouse serving as our bed and breakfast, I was happy to be away from the crowd. The cheery, elderly proprietors peeked blushingly around the corner as Erv picked me up and carried me across the threshold of our honeymoon suite. This romantic moment ended quickly as we then ran out to the car three more times to bring in our luggage and wedding gifts various friends had given us specifically for the "big night."

Once we had unloaded all of the loot, we changed out of the sweaty wedding clothes we'd been wearing for hours in the summer heat. It felt slightly awkward but we changed into comfy shorts and t-shirts so we could just relax. A private sitting area attached to our bedroom featured an inviting sofa so we both sat down nervously. Not sure what to do next, we decided to open our wedding cards. We read each one, blessed by the encouraging words and advice given by our loved ones.

As we opened each card, I collected the checks and Erv collected the cash. We honestly had low expectations since everyone had already given us so much to make the wedding a success. Once the last card was opened, we counted our individual stacks and then added them together. We could not believe the total. It was more money than either of us had ever seen at one time. The month-long honeymoon was on!

The big pile of cash gave us cause to celebrate! We both changed again, this time into something I would consider much less comfortable but apparently much more attractive. After a year of super-strict physical boundaries, it felt a little strange to suddenly have no limits at all—at least at first. Fortunately, this feeling didn't last very long.

I know movies show couples romantically falling asleep in each other's arms after they make love. This is what we both wanted to do. What the movies don't show you is that you probably want a towel nearby to clean up afterwards. For the ladies, you should also get up and go pee. This is the best way to avoid honeymoon cystitis.

A couple we know was honeymooning in Venice. They had to take an ambulance boat through the canals because it was the fastest way to the emergency room. The new wife had developed honeymoon cystitis (basically, a urinary tract infection) and needed antibiotics. We've known more than one couple who had a sexless honeymoon after the wedding night because the wife was in pain. This is easy to avoid. Here's your honeymoon strategy: sex, pee, sleep, repeat.

If you can't pee on demand you might want to try: drink, sex, pee, sleep, repeat. Fortunately we heard this advice before our honeymoon. No emergency room visits for us.

After our wedding night, we headed off for a week in New Hampshire at my cousin's cabin. The lakeside retreat offered countless opportunities for adventure. Beyond the obvious bedroom adventures (we called it "second-floor activity" because the first-floor windows had no curtains), the kitchen proved a source of curious exploration.

We'd never done much cooking together so this was a new source of fun. We'd travel to the nearby grocery store to pick out our ingredients and then bring our treasures home to make award-winning meals. Or at least we tried not to burn down the cabin. We soon discovered neither of us had much experience cooking grown-up food. Ramen noodles and mac 'n cheese are great for college, but they are not exactly honeymoon cuisine. But by the end of the week, we had both improved, enjoying some pretty tasty meals. And we only set off the smoke alarm twice.

We also enjoyed lots of inexpensive entertainment. We share a love of board games and had several "Risk" marathons. One morning, we started an intense match that lasted until dinnertime. There's nothing like world domination to bring romance into your new marriage. We also rented movies and spied on each other in the rustic outdoor shower. There was a zip-line outside, where we'd race to the lake's edge and plunge into the cool refreshing water. In between "second-floor activity" and trips to the bathroom, we'd have dance parties, hike nearby mountains, and explore the far edges of the lake by canoe. It was a very pleasant first week of marriage!

ERV'S TAKE

From honeymoon sex to board games, cooking, and the joys of the outdoors, there are many ways to enjoy one another without spending money you otherwise wouldn't have spent. When we play games together, we gain the benefit of looking into each other's eyes and having the chance to converse. Oh, we also have to wrestle with the competitive nature that comes out in both of us (it's on...game face...). During a movie we share similar emotions and the joy of cuddling. If the movie is great, we talk about it together. If not, then the movie can be abandoned and cuddling can build into second-floor activity. Sometimes I wish for a very bad movie!

A long walk is one of our favorite chances to discuss important life decisions, build intimacy through holding hands, and get a little movement in our day. Even a shower together can be a way to build intimacy and our comfort level by being naked together. We still cook together as a way to express love and develop creativity. I've always told Carrie that there are only a few things that occupy a man's mind (at least most of the time). They include: sex, food (I'm hungry right now), sleep, and sports. We can usually only focus on one at a time. So much for me being a multi-tasker.

What was a dream-like honeymoon for us might be a nightmare for you. We love simplicity and the outdoors. Our time at the cabin was actually the luxurious part of our one-month adventure. We slept in a bed, had a flushing toilet, an indoor stove, electricity, and hot water. These were common comforts we would be doing without for days at a time over the next three weeks. Our original honeymoon idea was a cross-country bike trip, which would have been even more rugged. Sore bottoms sounded like a bad idea for a honeymoon so we decided against it. A road trip camping expedition would be adventure enough for us.

Be sure to discuss your honeymoon expectations with your soon-to-be-spouse. Do you picture yourself relaxing somewhere tropical? Do you want to explore an exciting new city? What great adventure can you both enjoy? If your idea of a good time includes resort hotels and dining out, plan ahead to be sure you can afford it. If it's too expensive, think outside the box. Can you drive there instead of fly? Can you find a hotel including breakfast? There are always options. Exploring them together ensures you both have your expectations met.

Upon the conclusion of our time in New Hampshire, we loaded up our camping equipment and drove south. Little did we know our unconventional road-trip honeymoon would lay such a strong foundation for our marriage relationship. Traveling eight to fourteen hours a day by car provided wonderful opportunities for us to work on our communication. In the quintessential genre of a college road trip, we found ourselves trapped in a confined space forcing us to work through our difficulties. This is where we discovered one of our greatest marital challenges—reading a map.

A map is essential to a successful road trip. We had a good map. In fact, we had a few good maps. We also had a trip planner from AAA outlining our journey road-by- road, turn-by-turn. This, however, is only helpful if you stick to the planned route. Maybe this is our real problem. We both like to be spontaneous. If only we'd had a GPS in the summer of 1993, our honeymoon would have been spared much heartache.

We blissfully began our journey in New York State, heading

south through the Blue Ridge Mountains, and later found our-selves near Hot Springs, Arkansas. While our planned route did not take us directly to Hot Springs, we thought it would be a really neat place to experience. We ventured off course about an hour and drove into the town of Hot Springs.

This was our first mistake. We were greeted with big red, white, and blue banners declaring, "Boyhood Town of Bill Clin-ton," (the president at the time). This was great, but how about signs saying, "The Actual Hot Springs are This Way?" We never found those. In fact, after two hours of asking for directions, wandering around aimlessly, and asking for directions again, we became convinced there was not a single person in Hot Springs, Arkansas who actually knew where the Hot Springs were. We seriously doubt to this day they even exist.

After wasting three hours of our day searching in vain for hot springs, we decided to cut our losses and return to the road. We could drive the hour back to the interstate and still arrive at our next campsite by sundown. This was our plan. However, some-thing strange happened as we drove back to the highway. What should have taken only an hour was taking two hours, then three hours. I had somehow misread the route back and took us far off course. Erv was angry, and I felt miserable. The car was silent… for a very long time.

Being trapped in a car with an angry person is not fun. In fact, it is one of the worst kinds of torture a person can experi-ence. You cannot walk away. You cannot run and hide. A shout-ing match could cause an accident. The only option is silence. As previously mentioned, I have no talent for silence. And typically, Erv does not either. Long conversations of endless chatter are characteristically strengths of our relationship. But, when miles off course searching for an obscure campsite in the dark, Erv and I were masters of silence.

This was not the honeymoon bliss for which I was hoping. I had not imagined us arguing over a map. I never pictured us speaking harsh words to one another because we couldn't find an over-rated, well-hidden national landmark. I certainly hadn't dreamed of us driving hours side by side, less than a foot apart, in complete silence. It required all the self-control I possessed to not break down and cry.

In Erv's grandparents' borrowed red Subaru, I made a decision. This was an insignificant problem. Losing a few hours of drive time was not an important issue. There was no reason to stay upset. If our marriage was going to work—if I at least wanted to enjoy the remainder of my honeymoon—I could not stay upset. Small things needed to stay small things. I still loved Erv. I was quite sure he still loved me. He was frustrated and it was temporary. Tears were unnecessary. We were fine.

This is important to learn early in your marriage. An unexpected argument is not a reason to give up hope. As a couple, you're going to experience challenges completely out of your control. When these insignificant arguments start, it's easy to blow them out of proportion. You or your new spouse may speak words you don't mean. You may use a tone of voice showing complete disrespect for your partner. You will have a choice to make.

You can take a step back and recognize this is an insignificant argument. You can choose to keep small things small. It will always be tempting to make a grandiose deal of a small argument. You just might unleash all of your anger and frustration about every tiny issue annoying you about your spouse in that unexpected moment. What started miniscule can become huge and out of control quite quickly. This is an important time to exercise self-control.

Holding your tongue and staying calm is key. This is exactly what we did in the car after our misdirected trip. We were quiet and it was okay. We didn't run, because we couldn't, but we also chose not to attack. When we found our campsite, we calmly restarted our conversation. It was awkward and a little forced at first, but we were talking.

Fortunately for us, a good night's sleep changes everything. In fact, just being mutually horizontal makes for a quick improvement. Even though we had been married less than two weeks, we had already become accustomed to falling asleep in each other's arms. The thought of sleeping on the cold, hard ground with a chasm of silence between us was not appealing. By the time we were snuggled into our sleeping bags, we were laughing and teasing each other that, one day, we could brag to the world about visiting the boyhood town of Bill Clinton. All our friends would be totally jealous.

CHAPTER EIGHT

FOR BETTER OR FOR WORSE

Your honeymoon might be the first time you spend extended time alone together. Even if you've been dating for a while, there is something about being completely alone that allows you to connect in a new way. This is a rewarding time of discovery and exploration. When the two of you are alone, no one else defines you. You can completely decide who you are going to be as one. Establishing this connection forms a powerful bond between the two of you.

During this irreplaceable time, you'll discover aspects of each other's personality you hadn't seen before. Maybe you've never experienced each other first thing in the morning. This can be really amusing. Erv loves teasing my half-awake morning grogginess. Or, perhaps, you've never noticed what your partner is like when they're extremely hungry. This is when I'm most impatient and irritable. Extended time together allows you to see it all: the good, the bad, and the ugly.

There is a unique vulnerability that comes along with being married. You are no longer on your guard and your true colors really show. When you notice a refreshing sense of humor under pressure or keen ability to problem solve in your new spouse, it's a wonderful discovery. When some of his or her darker personality traits start to show, it can be challenging to accept.

When we're dating, we tend to focus on our similarities. We value the traits we share in common and celebrate them. They are often the foundation of our relationship. This was certainly true for us. Once we're married and we have extended time together, more and more of the differences start appearing. I saw our first major personality clash at Red Rock Canyon, a few days after our Hot Springs detour.

The Red Rock Canyon Campground was ridiculously inexpensive. We were so excited to be saving money, we quickly pulled into the vast expanse of red earth, surrounded by towering rock walls. We found our assigned site, a small square of dirt surrounded by several other small squares of dirt with tents on them. There was no shade whatsoever. We spread out our tent just as the wind picked up. It blew our tent like a sail, and it almost ripped right out of our hands. I tried to hold it steady while Erv tried pounding in the tent stakes. The ground was as hard as a rock. In fact, the ground was rock. Red rock. It was impenetrable. Erv tried and tried to pound in those stakes.

In the meantime, I only had two arms. While I would hold down two corners of the tent, the other half of the tent would blow wildly in the wind. Erv got more and more frustrated as the blowing tent flapped in his face while the red rock ground refused to succumb to his pounding.

In general, I don't get frustrated easily. While I found our situation challenging, it did not make me particularly angry. If anything, our sail of a tent was slightly amusing. I tried to keep things laid back and easy going. Everyone else had their tents up around us. Surely there was a way we could succeed. It was simply a matter of time. Erv, however, became so frustrated, he picked the flying tent up over his head, ready to send it crashing into the enormous walls of Red Rock Canyon. It was at this moment I yelled over the roaring wind, "It's not our tent!" This little reminder seemed to bring him back to his senses.

Once Erv calmed down, I pointed out that we could put our bags inside the tent. This would keep it from blowing away while we managed to secure it to the ground. We were both amused at this obvious solution, unsure why it hadn't occurred to us earlier.

This brief episode was the first of many where our differing personalities made themselves apparent. When this happens to you, don't be discouraged. It can be unsettling to see darker aspects of your partner's personality for the first time. Don't be freaked when you see your new spouse act in a way that surprises you. Marriage is full of surprises. Embrace them as opportunities to know and love your partner more fully. Remember, you married them for better or for worse. The worse in both of you will come out sooner or later.

While I appreciate when Erv demonstrates patience and self-control, I'm glad he doesn't feel the need to hide his feelings of frustration from me. I don't want him to pretend everything is okay when it's not. I can be a much more supportive wife when I know what's bothering him. He does the same for me when I'm tired or hungry.

Learning these differences also allows you to be more effective in your communication. When I notice Erv is getting frustrated, I don't ask him a lot of annoying questions. I also don't laugh out loud at his angry antics, although sometimes

I want to. Erv doesn't ask me to do critical thinking or planning when I first wake up or when I haven't eaten in a while. I won't make good decisions or give him helpful feedback at these times. When you're on a journey to live as one, you find ways to accommodate each other's strengths and weaknesses.

Discovering each other's strengths is one of the greatest adventures of marriage. My husband is a courageous risk taker. I've experienced incredible voyages I would have never dared try without Erv's encouragement. When you choose to live as one, you greatly benefit from the strengths of your spouse.

Both Erv and I always thought it would be awesome to camp in the Grand Canyon. We inquired about this when we arrived at the Grand Canyon park office a few days after our stay at Red Rock Canyon. We learned you needed to make reservations months in advance to camp in the canyon. Meanwhile, Erv was determined to at least see the Colorado River up close and personal. We asked about taking a donkey ride down and back. This was expensive and far outside of our budget. While it was tempting to say, "This is a once in a lifetime experience. Let's just charge it and pay it off later," we would not compromise our commitment to the honeymoon we could afford with the cash we had.

We decided to take a short, exploratory hike down into the canyon to check out the more affordable option—hiking by foot. We knew it would be demanding, but the price was right. We passed several signs warning hikers in big, bold letters not attempt a hike to the river and back in one day. They listed the number of people who had to be airlifted out and those who had died of dehydration. It sounded pretty serious to me. My new husband was (and still is) not good at following directions.

When you tell him not to do something, it's as if you asked him to please, please do it.

ERV'S TAKE

There is this common phrase, "once in a lifetime," that we apply to so many opportunities and decisions in life. Fortunately for Carrie and me, one of our mentors once said to me, "Erv, I've lived long enough to know, once in a lifetime opportunities often come around more than once in a lifetime." Sure enough we've had the opportunity to return to the Grand Canyon. Sometimes the adventure comes through taking the route less traveled, advised, or allowed.

I must tell you I have a simple risk-taking philosophy (I'm not an adrenaline junkie, but maybe secretly wish I was). My rule is: if someone else has done it and survived (truthfully they couldn't have gotten hurt either, because I am pain intolerant) then I'm in.

One of my favorite hot summer day activities is jumping off bridges, cliffs, ropes, etc… into water. I almost never go first. So, when I heard that others had hiked to the Colorado River and back in a day and survived, I had my answer. The only question, "Would my new wife come with me or not?" Fortunately for me, she did. It is an adventure we love to tell and a memory that bonds us together.

I guess there is nothing quite like an adventure that ends in joint dry-heaving to make a lasting impression and bond two hearts together. It is probably the reason other respected marriage advisors highly recommend camping. Something is bound to go wrong and that shared struggle builds your marriage bond in a powerful way—much like a scar that pulls your skin back together and makes it stronger than before. I'm not advocating pursuing pain for pain's sake, but when it comes, know you have the opportunity to grow closer through it.

Later the same day, while enjoying a hike along the rim of the canyon (a perfectly safe and beautiful way to experience the canyon, in my opinion), we passed a father and his grown sons. They were talking about hiking to the river and back the day before. Not at all embarrassed at having eavesdropped on their conversation, Erv proceeded to ask them what time they left, how much food and water they took with them, and how long the journey had taken them.

Erv was determined to go. I could stay back if I wanted to, but he was taking this chance. We didn't know when we'd ever make it back to the Grand Canyon. We'd driven all this way. He was not coming this close to the Colorado River and going home without experiencing it. His mind was made up.

Again, I had a choice to make. I could play it safe and hang out at the rim. Take another nice, little day hike along with the thousands of other tourists. Or I could do what few people were willing to do. I could take a risk and enjoy a great adventure with my new husband. It was an easy decision. I joined his river quest.

The trip down was pretty easy. It was actually a lot of fun. We practically ran down to stay ahead of the donkey tours and their donkey droppings. We stopped and refilled our canteens at the two planned water stops along the way. By 10 a.m., we were at the Colorado River. We accomplished our goal, and Erv was victorious. The river was much colder than we expected and the current was swift. Our images of playing in the water together quickly disappeared since we could not safely go in past our knees.

Then we encountered our first sign of trouble. Our canteens were just about empty, and we had no way to filter the water in the river for drinking. The first water stop on the way up was three miles away. No big deal, we thought. We can go three miles without much water.

By the time we packed up our bags and left the river, it was 11 a.m. We started the long, steep climb out of the canyon. Switchback after switchback, the desert sun beat down on us, covering us both with sweat. By noon it was more than 100 degrees, and I was begging Erv for water. We had so little left, he started rationing it. He would count to five as I drank and then pull the canteen away. He stopped drinking completely to make sure there would be enough for me.

By 1 p.m, we still were not at the water stop, and I was sure we would never make it out of this God-forsaken canyon alive. I could see myself pictured on the oversized warning posters. I will perish in the Grand Canyon on my honeymoon. With his hand on the small of my back, Erv started pushing me up the steep canyon path as I had lost the will to move forward.

As the temperature continued to climb, we ran out of water completely. Erv tried diligently to make it last, but it was impossible. I started to worry about him as he stopped drinking long before I had. The path began to level out, and we found ourselves entering the "Indian Garden" section of the canyon. This plateau is covered with beautiful varieties of cactus. It's the only patch of green standing in stark contrast to the red and brown rock all around you. More importantly, this is the location of the water stop. We had finally made it! There were dozens of people there, hot, tired, and thirsty like us, waiting for their turn at the single water spigot. When we finally filled our canteens, the water was the most refreshing drink on earth.

It was another three miles of climbing out of the next section of canyon. At least this time we were starting with full canteens. Erv continued rationing so we would not run out before the next water stop. The heat did not let up, and the switchbacks stretched out endlessly before us. Why were we doing this again? Erv and I had climbed several mountains together and had never experienced this. Mentally, it was a completely different strategy. When you climb a mountain, you do your hard work first, reach your destination, and enjoy the easy descent. The canyon was the opposite. We had all our fun in the beginning, enjoyed our reward, and then began the hard work of climbing out.

This challenging experience is the perfect analogy for our commitment against debt. Going into debt is like climbing to the bottom of the Grand Canyon. You have all of the fun in the beginning, you reach your desired goal, and then you begin the surprisingly hard work of paying it off … with interest (which is kind of like climbing in the heat while running out of water).

We had decided as a married couple that we wanted our financial lives to be more like climbing a mountain. We would do the hard work and make sacrifices in the beginning so that later we could achieve our goals and enjoy life without the heavy burden of debt.

ERV'S TAKE

So Carrie took so much more from our Grand Canyon experience than I did. For me, the adventure was a no cost way to create a powerful memory and bond. It does also relate to the idea of debt well. It is so fun to buy something new and bring it home. It's like Christmas morning, only any day you choose, and you got to select just the "right" present for yourself. But, when that purchase is made with tomorrow's money then the story is incomplete. You should feel great at that moment, if not then you really made a mistake and bad purchase – return the items as soon as you can.

What we are encouraging is for you to think about the joy of today versus the cost of tomorrow. Because credit allows you to experience the joy more separated from the cost, it is easier to get ourselves into trouble. We feel good now and don't feel badly until we are paying on something that now feels old and has lost its luster and appeal. It is a bit like drinking (I am not advocating this, by the way) where the feel-good is on the front end and the feel-bad comes later. So, I recommend one simple question: Would I buy this for cash? No? Then don't buy it on credit. Yes? Then buy it with cash.

We reached the second water stop and rested a short while before the final ascent to the rim. By now it was mid-afternoon. We were in danger of being stranded in the canyon after dark. Erv and I were determined to make it out in the light. We were also growing hungry, having run out of food.

My favorite food on the planet is ice cream. I believe the world would be a happier place if everyone ate ice cream daily. My new husband was well aware of my obsession and used this to motivate me. If we got back to the canyon ridge by 5 p.m., he would buy me ice cream. It was 3:30 p.m., and we were both completely exhausted. On a good day, three miles of uphill climbing could be accomplished easily. On a 100 degree day after hours of grueling climbing, I was skeptical, but determined. The promise of ice cream somehow gave me a second wind, and now I was climbing ahead of Erv, encouraging him to keep up with me.

As we neared the top, he was really dragging. "You're not going to make me miss ice cream, buddy," I called back to him. I made it to the top with five minutes to spare. Though we were completely exhausted and dehydrated when the climb was over, we celebrated our victorious expedition. We successfully hiked eighteen miles in the scorching dessert of the Grand Canyon and reached the beautiful Colorado River as a team. It was an incredible feeling, forging a strong bond between us as newlyweds.

I would never have attempted this hike apart from Erv's courageous defiance. This was the first of many times in our marriage when I would experience something extraordinary thanks to borrowing Erv's strength. Likewise, Erv has come to depend on my patience and positive attitude to see him through challenging circumstances. Marriage allows you to draw on the assets of your partner in ways benefitting you both.

CHAPTER NINE

FUND FUTURE ADVENTURES

I am a huge fan of living in the moment. Being present with those you love, today, allows you to focus your attention and affection on them. However, there are certain seasons of your life when it's wise to spend some time planning for the future. The beginning of your marriage is an important time to consider and make plans for your life together for years to come.

One of the first decisions you'll make as a newlywed couple is how to spend the generous wedding money you receive. If you want to establish your marriage on a firm foundation of financial stability, be smart with how you use this unique gift of cash. Instead of simply focusing on your present needs, think about your future together. This is an excellent opportunity to begin saving as a couple. By putting this money into a savings account, you give yourself peace of mind. Unexpected expenses will come your way. When you have money set aside in savings, these emergencies are far less stressful on your marriage.

When you have no savings, you have no protection against

unfortunate circumstances. Car repairs, injuries, and loss of work are realities of adult life. Once you're married, you are responsible for the welfare of two people, not just one. Putting money into savings allows you to provide for yourself and your spouse. This is not only responsible, but it also demonstrates love to your partner.

If one or both of you already had a healthy savings account before your marriage, you can consider other options with this money. Perhaps you want to invest it so it can multiply over time. The younger you are when you begin investing, the more time your money has to double. Through the life of your marriage, this can really add up.

If you enter your marriage with debt, paying this off should be a high priority. Debt puts an unnecessary strain on your relationship. While we would have enjoyed buying new furniture or taking an exotic vacation with our wedding money, instead we chose to pay off our school loans. And we paid our car insurance for a year. It wasn't very glamorous, but starting our life together with absolutely no debt was a freeing feeling that greatly blessed our marriage.

ERV'S TAKE

If you plan to have a retirement account, the money you put into the account in your 20's is much more valuable at the time that you retire than the money put in during your 30's and 40's. Starting early is key to growing your retirement. Even if you don't plan to build a retirement account, you should think about the future as well as the present with your finances.

If you own a car, it will need to be repaired and eventually replaced. If you own a home it will need maintenance, renovations, or new furnishings. Putting a little away for these "known" but future expenses makes it easier to pay them when the time comes. Then there are the unexpected life realities, e.g. one of you gets sick or your hours at work get cut. Many financial advisors (and we agree) recommend 3-6 months of money in an emergency fund for such possibilities. If you can't get 3-6 months right away, then start with a goal of getting $1,000 in an emergency account. We hope you won't need this money, but life, friends, family, and countless acquaintances confirm that for most of us, we will need an emergency fund from time to time.

Current debt usually means paying interest. You can think of that interest as a way for you to earn a return. Right now our bank is paying us .1% interest on our money. That's 1/10th of a percent! So, if I have a credit card with 11% (not bad for a credit card) or 18% or more percent interest AND I have some money in the bank then…. I could pay some or all of that credit card bill off and be "earning/saving" 11% or 18% versus the .1% my bank is paying me. Pay off your high interest debts with the money you have (even if that means only a small extra payment each month to begin with).

Should you set up an emergency fund or pay off your credit cards? My advice is to split the money you could save or pay on the car (50/50 to start). If you can save $30 a week, put $15 in an emergency fund (.1%) and $15 extra toward your debt payment. Once you reach $1,000 in your emergency fund, then you can pay the full $30 on your credit cards/debt.

Now is also the perfect time to create a spending plan for your new family. Many people call this a budget. You can give it whatever name you like. We like "spending plan" because this is a chance for you to decide how you want to spend your money. Don't see establishing a budget or spending plan as a chore. It's an opportunity to determine your priorities as a couple and reflect them as a couple.

When we first established our spending plan, it was challenging. The teaching job I wanted never materialized. I entered the market along with a surplus of newly educated teachers. There were more than 200 applicants for each job available. Even though I had excellent references and a passion for teaching, I didn't have experience or a master's degree. Schools were looking for someone with both. This left me with the option of substitute teaching, an unpredictable source of income.

Erv was a full-time graduate student. He was willing to work but needed to find something accommodating him being out of town part of the week for classes. He also wanted to find something in youth ministry. Our church approached us with a plan resulting in an amazing answer to prayer.

After working as summer youth interns in the past, our

church was interested in hiring us to serve as youth pastors for one full year. We could both work part-time and together we would collect a full-time salary. The job was going to greatly help our financial situation. With a predictable income from the church, we made up a monthly spending plan according to our modest youth pastor salary. Any additional income from my substitute teaching would go directly into savings. We chose to not count on it for monthly expenses.

We recommend this as a strategy for most young couples. If you can live on only one income, even if it means making financial sacrifices, it would be wise for you to do so. Plan your monthly spending around one income and plan to save the other. Put this away toward one-time expenses such as a car or home purchase.

Before you have children, you have the unique ability to maximize your earning potential. Without extra mouths to feed, childcare expenses, and other related costs, you can live quite simply as a newlywed couple. Enjoy this time and consider living on less than you need instead of always spending as much as you're able. Everything you can save now will bless your marriage later when there is greater pressure due to a growing family.

We recommend you start by creating a monthly spending plan based on one income. Calculate your rent or mortgage payment, utilities, groceries, car expenses, clothing, giving, and entertainment . You may have other categories you want to add. You can track this with an online budgeting program, an Excel spreadsheet, or simple pen and paper. Employ whatever method you will consistently use.

When we were first married, we wrote our spending plan category names on envelopes and put the allotted amount into the envelopes each month. When the envelope was empty, we would have to stop spending money in that category.

After awhile, the envelope system became cumbersome. Once we were pretty well trained as to our financial limits, we switched to keeping track of expenses by category on a piece of paper. There would be a column for each category, and we would subtract from the total whenever we spent money. This piece of paper later became an Excel spreadsheet. We kept track of everything from donations at church to milkshakes at McDonalds. We still use this method today.

Keeping track of your expenses is critical to success with your budget. If you don't keep track of your spending, it's hard to know if you're overspending. Establish the habit of writing down your expenses early on in your marriage. Keep receipts or keep a small log in your bag. If you frequently shop with a credit or debit card, you can find programs online to track your spending according to your goals. Don't make excuses to not do this. Unless you are independently wealthy, you need to monitor your use of money.

If one of you is better at keeping track of these details than the other, this is a meaningful way for you to contribute to your marriage. Tracking our finances is a strength of Erv's and he does a wonderful job monitoring our spending. It is important, however, for you both to be involved in this process. It is too large a burden for one person to carry alone. Make sure you both know your spending goals and limits. You both need to take responsibility for sticking to the budget you established together, even if one of you holds the primary responsibility to pay the bills and manage your financial accounts.

It's essential for you to sit down as a couple every few months and look at your spending plan. See if you're staying on track with your goals. Is there an area where you are always over-spending? You may need to adjust your spending habits. These decisions should be made together.

Sometimes you may find you have different priorities with how you want to spend your money. Maybe one of you loves to play golf or buy clothes. Perhaps one of you really enjoys giving and the other really enjoys saving. Your spending plan needs to reflect your priorities as a couple. Strive to find a balance between both of your needs recognizing your money as a shared resource. By setting these priorities early in your marriage, you allow your money to bring you together as a couple instead of driving you apart.

When our budget was looking tight during our first year of marriage, we could look back at our written record and find out exactly where we were overspending. Keeping track of expenses kept us both openly communicating about our wants and needs when it came to money. When we disagreed about a purchase, we had the common ground of our spending plan to stand on. It saved us from typical marriage arguments about money.

The decisions we made about money at the beginning of our marriage defined the future we are living today. Our historic home, international trips, and meaningful careers were all made possible by the decisions we made to live simply in those early years of our marriage. It you want to live a life of adventure in the future, endeavor to live on less than you make today so you have money to do all you dream of. Your future self will thank you for having been so darn smart at the beginning of journey!

CHAPTER TEN

SEX, DATING AND OTHER MARRIAGE MISSIONS

When you write something down, it tells your mind it's important.

Every married couple should begin their marriage by writing out a mission statement. A mission statement is your proclamation of purpose as a couple. What do you want your future together to look like? What will bring your marriage greater meaning in the future? It's important to write these goals out. If you aim at nothing, you'll hit it every time.

It's important to take some time early on in your marriage to write out your priorities. Hopefully, you've already done this in regard to your money. Your budget tells you your financial priorities. Your marriage mission statement tells you how you want to invest your time and energy as a couple.

When we were first married, Erv and I wanted to move forward as a couple with a sense of purpose and intentionality. We believed that putting our purpose on paper would guide us toward our shared goals and vision.

After talking for several hours about our hopes and dreams as a couple, we came up with the following statement for the new Starr Family. Here is our mission statement composed in 1993. Warning: it's long!

"As a family we commit to work as a team, demonstrating in our relationship with each other and those around us the character of Christ by encouraging, sharpening, teaching, learning, listening to, and loving one another. To help meet the needs of those we encounter to the best of our ability.

To live focused on today, with the recognition that this moment may be all we have—before the time we are called to give an account to our Lord and Savior Jesus Christ. To be ready at all times to share and live the message of Jesus. To share all that we have been given and to be good stewards.

To serve and minister to students. To raise our children to be leaders who strive to be like Jesus. To laugh often and keep a positive, hopeful outlook. To cry with those who cry and are hurting. To be open and honest with each other and God. To provide a safe place for those in need. To strive always to know God, each other, and the world in which we minister better. To remain debt free. To conquer fears and to seek justice and truth."

Once you write out and finalize your mission statement, I recommend printing it out and posting it somewhere you can regularly see it. Some friends of ours commissioned a family member to write their statement in calligraphy. Then they framed it and displayed it in their home as a piece of art. What a powerful daily reminder of their united purpose.

Looking back at our mission statement twenty years after we wrote it, it's amazing to see how much we have stayed true to our original goals. These statements still characterize who we are as a family today. What kind of legacy would you like to leave behind as a couple?

Having our mission written out as newlyweds guided the use of our time and our money. Just as the budget gave us common ground from which we could make decisions, so did our mission statement. This was important as we soon learned there would always be pressing demands that challenge our priorities.

Shortly after we were married, my work as a substitute teacher picked up quickly. Within weeks, I was asked to teach every day. I was hired for maternity leave after maternity leave, keeping me busy from 6 a.m. to 6 p.m. daily. We had weekly prayer meetings and outreach events with the youth group. We also taught Sunday school, planned retreats, and hosted parent meetings.

With all of this busyness, we saw the need to establish a weekly date night so our marriage wouldn't get lost in the commotion. We chose one night a week where we would not plan anything except time with each other. We guarded this time as sacred ground. If someone else asked us to do something at that time, we always said no. We had to say no a lot. We still do.

Because we were trying to live on one income during our newlywed years, we tried to capitalize on creativity instead of cash to enjoy a variety of "in-dates." We played lots of cards (especially pinochle) and board games we'd received as wedding gifts. We also enjoyed candlelight dinners and backyard picnics. These were especially romantic when I managed not to burn our meal. (I was still learning how to cook real food.)

Sharing life together is a blessing. It is one of the joys and rewards of marriage and family. We encourage you to make the "normal" aspects of life a means to communicate love, build intimacy, and make good financial decisions. There is always a more expensive way to have a similar experience. Sometimes we choose that more expensive avenue. But, we don't want to lose sight of how much we enjoy each other – somewhat in spite of what we are doing or how much we're spending.

ERV'S TAKE

Do you remember how much you enjoyed simply being together at the beginning of your relationship? That doesn't have to change. You can grab a lunch and have a picnic and the memory of the experience will likely be more rewarding than a meal at a fine restaurant. Not that I have anything against a well-prepared meal out, it is truly a pleasure to eat something you don't (or maybe even can't) make on your own.

Sometimes money becomes the avenue of the lazy. I've resembled this remark myself—I let someone else do the planning and work, and I'll just pay for it. Sometimes this is the best choice, but it isn't the only choice. Take a walk down memory lane and think of the simple ways you used to enjoy each other's company when you had less and life was simpler. Ask yourself "What can we do today that I'll want to tell my grandchildren about in years to come?" This is why Carrie and I sometimes end up playing outside during a downpour, enjoying a little mud sliding adventure.

In that first year of marriage, our best "in-dates" came on the nights when Erv would return home after being gone at seminary for a few days. I always planned a special homecoming. I would put signs up around the house, cook a special dessert, or have his favorite music playing. The best homecoming was when I left him clues for a scavenger hunt. I waited patiently hidden in our bedroom closet while Erv made his way around the house searching for the next clue. When he finally found me, we didn't need television or even board games to keep us entertained. Scavenger hunts became Erv's favorite way to be welcomed home.

Don't let being married stop you from dating and enjoying playfulness in your marriage. When we're dating, it's easy to put a lot of energy into the relationship. We go out of our way to make our time together extra special. Once we get married, it's easy to take your relationship for granted. Many couples stop investing effort into their marriage shortly after the honeymoon. They don't make time for just the two of them and they slowly grow apart.

Keep dating and put effort into your time together. Be fun and spontaneous. We love to get in the car and just drive, not knowing where we'll end up. When we're out on the motorcycle together, this is especially fun. But don't be lazy in the name of spontaneity. Investing some time into planning special outings now and then speaks volumes to your spouse about how important they are.

If you see yourself getting into the habit of going to the same exact restaurant or always going out to the movies, make a point to change it up. It's fine to have a few special places you go to regularly. There are some restaurants we consider "ours" because we frequent them so often. But, we make a point to infuse the routine of our favorites with new experiences as often as possible. By switching up the environment, we also stimulate new conversation, fresh ideas, and breathe energy into our relationship.

Energize your relationship with adventure. Make your dates exciting! Go do something together that gets your heart racing. Drive to an amusement park and ride all the rollercoasters. Rent some jet skis at a nearby lake. Pull off to the side of the road, blast the music and have a dance party up on the hood of your car. Don't always play it safe. Love is a risk. Take some risks together.

Also, be sure to make time and space for physical intimacy. Sex is the glue holding married couples together. It's the one experience you share together that is completely unique from every other relationship you have. The more attention you give to your sex life, the better your marriage relationship will be.

There are so many ways you can improve your physical intimacy as a couple. Take time to leave a note on your wife's pillow in the morning. Send your husband a quick text saying you look forward to him coming home. Sit closer than necessary at the dinner table. Don't be afraid to flirt and joke with one another. These little moments all contribute to a closer bond and a better sex life.

One of the easiest ways to improve your married sex life is to go to bed earlier. Too many couples neglect physical intimacy because they're too tired. I'm pretty sure you weren't too tired on your honeymoon. Don't let sex become a chore you're too exhausted to enjoy. Go to bed before you're completely worn out. Leave yourself some time to be together before you fall asleep.

Some of the best marriage advice we ever received was to sleep naked. While this may seem awkward or uncomfortable, it will do wonders for your relationship. It's hard to stay angry when you aren't wearing clothes. Whatever the argument is about, it all seems less important when you're naked.

Sleeping naked also keeps you vulnerable. Removing the barrier of clothes is a daily reminder to remove whatever barriers you've put up between you and your spouse. You'll also be warmer at night. Body heat is better than a blanket. We own pajamas for Christmas morning and emergencies only. With your clothes already off, you will have sex more often. We believe quantity equals quality here because practice makes perfect. Sleeping naked will help your sex life go from good to great! Don't let sex become a special occasion in your marriage. Instead let it be part of your daily experience together as a couple.

One major hindrance to enjoying your sex life as a married couple is concerns about pregnancy. With weekly "reunions" and no television for the whole first year of our marriage, birth control became an important consideration. Our discussions about birth control actually began long before we got married. Erv and I were both interested in someday having children. In fact, we wanted a whole bunch of children. But we both agreed it would be best if we waited for a few years. First, we wanted to save some money and buy a house. If we saved all of my income and lived only on Erv's salary, it would take about five years to buy a modest house for cash. After talking with a few trusted families from church, we decided that natural family planning was our preferred method to postpone having children.

This particular method of birth control was new to us. Our friends gave us a book that explained in detail what we needed to do. Basically, we would learn when I was ovulating during each month and abstain from sex during that time. It seemed simple and straightforward.

The best part of natural family planning is that it is completely and totally free. There are no purchases to be made, prescriptions to be refilled, or procedures to be paid for. The difficult part of natural family planning is that it requires lots of self-control. To successfully employ NFP, you must be well disciplined and have good communication as a couple. After our year of purity and three years of friendship, we'd become pretty good at both. We found NFP to be a very effective method of birth control— as long as we stuck to the plan.

Did I mention that Erv and I both like to be spontaneous?

For our first year of marriage, NFP worked very well. We kept careful track of the days we could enjoy each other and the days we were likely to get pregnant. This became a routine we were both familiar with as we'd ask one another, "Are we in a safe zone," before we'd allow things to go too far. Usually this was no big deal, but what about special occasions? Anniversaries, birthdays, and weekly reunions didn't always fall into a "safe zone." We both started pushing the envelope on our "safe zones" until the recommended seven days of abstinence was whittled down to three. Just weeks after our first anniversary, I was "surprisingly" pregnant.

CHAPTER ELEVEN

THE CEMENT OF SHARED SUFFERING

Very few things in life go according to our plans. This is especially true in marriage. We bring so many expectations to the table. Most of us hope our marriage partner will make our lives complete. If only we had someone to share everything with, we would be fulfilled. Unfortunately, that's an awful lot of pressure to put on one person.

When life is going well and everything is happening as we expect, it's easy to appreciate and value our spouse. We see all the good they do and we celebrate it. However, when life throws us a curve ball, the person closest to us easily becomes the enemy. I've always found this incredibly perplexing. Why do we give the worst treatment to those who are closest to us?

It's easiest for us to take for granted those we know will love us anyway. There's something about knowing they will eventually forgive us. We grant ourselves silent permission to mistreat them. We say and do things we wouldn't say or do to anyone else.

Proximity alone makes it difficult to always be on our best

behavior. At some point we need to let our guard down and just be ourselves. This is most likely to happen at home. It's difficult to be disciplined and self-controlled at the time—especially with our words and attitude.

It's also easiest to attack and hurt those close to us because we know all of their weaknesses. When you open yourself up to your partner, you make yourself incredibly vulnerable. This is necessary for a close and healthy relationship, but it's also risky. Those closest to you know where all of the chinks in your armor can be found. When you're upset, it's easy to attack your partner where you know it hurts the most.

This is what happened to us when we discovered we were pregnant. Our relationship turned downright ugly. Though we were both fully responsible for this unexpected blessing, it was not what either of us had planned. After a year of substituting for women on maternity leave, I was finally a prime candidate for my own classroom. In the meantime, Erv had decided to not finish his third year of seminary. While the church was willing to hire us for another year of youth ministry, I expected teaching full time to be challenging enough, and Erv was no longer interested in pursuing ministry. The church hired someone else, and my teaching job didn't materialize (again). I left substitute teaching to work as a migrant teacher and decided to begin a master's degree. Erv got a low paying job at a home for special needs children. Our five-year savings plan came to a screeching halt.

All of these changes disheartened both of us. I enjoyed my new teaching position, working in classrooms to help the children of migrant farmers. But now that I was pregnant, my dream of one day having my own classroom would be further delayed.

Once the baby arrived, I didn't want to be working full time for at least a few years.

ERV'S TAKE

We learned quickly that life does not always go as you hoped or planned. God provides, but often we need to adjust our agenda to follow His. We benefited from a common principle of living on what we earned (or less), and trying not to be dependent on both of us earning full-time incomes (since we have seldom both been able to do so). We need to plan for the unexpected. Sometimes that is an unexpected opportunity and success; sometimes it means unexpected challenges and learning to walk by faith.

The opportunity to learn and grow comes in many forms. For me, it meant learning to work with children who were severely disabled. It taught me about the blessings of "everyday" things: life, health, running, and speech. The children taught me about joy, love, and contentment. My co-workers taught me patience, compassion, and humility. These were valuable lessons, forged in a setting not of my own choosing, but an effective classroom all the same.

After a year of enjoying carefree marital bliss, our lives became stressed and our relationship strained. Our collective and individual dreams were falling apart. I worked all day traveling between three school districts while attending graduate school three nights a week. Erv worked the overnight shift, which meant we rarely saw each other. We kept to our meager budget, but paying cash for grad school meant our rate of savings was minimal.

My ultimate dream had always been having children. I wanted so much to be excited about this new baby. One of my best friends had a one-year-old, and I enjoyed spending time with her and her son. The special bond they shared was one I'd always looked forward to. And I knew Erv would be the kind of father I had always wanted growing up. I thought we would make a great parenting team. Unfortunately, the timing of the pregnancy seemed to be ruining everything.

One evening when I was finished with my night class, Erv and I went out for a walk. It was cool and dark and the first chill of fall hung in the air. These nighttime walks admiring the stars had always been a relaxing time for us to enjoy. This particular night, we felt more like enemies than friends. We blamed each other for this "mistake" and the consequences we were now facing. Our whole timeframe was ruined, and our future had become completely uncertain. We both made rash statements we didn't mean. By the time we got home, I was in tears. Desperate for peace to return to our lives, I secretly prayed this pregnancy would end and our lives could return to normal.

I woke up early the next morning with extreme abdominal pain. Hours passed, and it would not subside. I asked Erv to take me to the hospital. He called our pastor and his wife, who met us at the emergency room. They prayed for us as doctors and nurses flitted in and out of my sterile, curtained area. They gave me a barrage of tests as my mind prepared for the worse. I pleaded with God to ignore my desperate prayer from the night before. We patiently waited for the test results. Finally, a grim-faced doctor entered the room and pulled his chair up alongside my bed.

"Your ultrasound shows no signs of life. I'm sorry. You should go home and get some rest."

My mind searched for an alternate meaning to his words— Was there no hope at all? Could he possibly be wrong? Were there more tests they should perform? As I asked my questions, the doctor confirmed my fears: our baby was gone. In a matter of moments, I'd gone from an expectant mother to an empty shell. As I slipped into the bathroom to change into my clothes, I wept bitter tears of regret.

Erv and I returned to our apartment in silence. Word of our miscarriage traveled quickly, and friends stopped by with flowers and food. I didn't want to see anyone. The phone rang, but we ignored it. I didn't want to talk to anyone. We sat alone in the dark. Within hours, the abdominal cramping grew worse. I sat in the middle of the living room floor with Erv's arms wrapped around me. The physical and emotional pain engulfed me like a dark cloud. We prayed and held each other, feeling the loss of a gift for which we'd shown little thankfulness.

As we struggled through the night, we clung to each other. By morning, we were exhausted and resigned to the truth that we could not bring our baby back. We spent the day alone in our apartment again, repenting of our ungrateful hearts. All throughout the week, friends continued to bring us meals, flowers, and encouraging notes. As we read their words, we received their comfort and accepted God's forgiveness.

At the end of the week, Erv and I took a hike to one of our favorite spots, Nichols Tower. As the sun shone on our faces, we reflected on Psalm 30:5, "Weeping may stay for the night, but rejoicing comes in the morning." We determined morning had come. Though our sadness remained, we would rejoice in our blessings and the future God had for us. We trusted He would give us children in His time.

When we go through difficult times together, it bonds us in a powerful way. There is something significant about suffering through the same trial with another human being. As we journey through it together, our emotions become so raw. We utter words we wouldn't dream of speaking out loud. We express thoughts we typically keep hidden. We share fears and worries without reservation.

There is an intimacy that builds around shared struggle. We sit closer. We wrap an arm around a shoulder. We grasp one another's hands. We embrace and hang on just a little longer than is socially acceptable. But the desperation of the moment makes it okay. It becomes necessary. We are surviving and human touch reminds us we are still alive.

When you go through this as a couple, it is a gift. It can also be a test. In the midst of the struggle, it's easy to turn on one another. We can make our spouse the enemy instead of our partner. There is always the temptation to run to someone outside of our marriage for comfort. In our desire to escape the challenge, we seek refuge in a stranger or a friend. This is a missed opportunity. There is no better time to turn to your spouse—even if they have failed you in the past. You have promised to love them for a lifetime. They have committed to stand by and support you through all of life's circumstances. Give them another chance to do that.

If you aren't intentional about supporting your partner in times of difficulty, a chasm of hurt will grow between the two of you. Watching your partner suffer is incredibly painful. It's torture, really. You just want to take the pain away, no matter what. You want to bear their burden for them. If you're uncertain of how to support your spouse when they are hurting, try anyway. Don't be afraid of making a mistake in the way you comfort them. It would be worse for you to simply move on as if the difficulty didn't happen. Don't rush back into life as usual. You need to feel the struggle together. Don't miss the opportunity to grow closer together through shared pain.

Once you emerge from the challenge and the dust settles, you will share the same wounds and scars. You will have stories to share and victories to celebrate. The memories will be precious when you look back. It will energize and strengthen your marriage. After losing our first baby, Erv and I enjoyed a new sense of closeness. We had suffered and survived together. This bond became the firm foundation we would stand on during the trials and challenges to come.

CHAPTER TWELVE

BROKEN DREAMS AND SHATTERED GLASS

After the extreme sadness of our loss, we were less than committed to preventing pregnancy. We weren't intentionally trying to get pregnant, but apparently, we don't have to. Within months of losing our first baby, we were pregnant with our second.

Life had just started returning to normal. We were both still working low paying jobs, paying for grad school, and trying to save all we could. Motivated to increase our earnings, Erv took another part-time job, and we invested in a multi-level marketing company. We attended rallies, sold products, and encouraged friends and family members to join our new business. With Erv's head for numbers and my sales savvy, we were off to a strong start. Within months, we were setting records within the company. We were the bright shining stars of our network. Surely we would advance quickly and fast track our way to our life goals.

Unfortunately, as we returned to our family mission statement, we found ourselves convicted. We were spending every free moment promoting our business. Every conversation was focused on achieving success. Every relationship became a potential "contact." The money we were investing in products and promotional material was consuming the majority of our profit. This business was costing us financially as well as emotionally. By spring, we became inactive in our new company. This was a significant decision, but after talking and praying together, we agreed this was the right move for us. Erv's next decision, however, took me completely by surprise.

A failed businessman, an underpaid worker, and an expectant father, Erv was desperate for a change. We gave our landlords notice that we would be moving out in thirty days. We were moving to Albany where we could be closer to Erv's family, and he could pursue an MBA. I was disappointed and angry. Oneonta was our home. Our friends and church family were here. My migrant teaching job was here. My graduate school was here. I couldn't possibly pick up in the middle of all that and move.

This was a real challenge for me as a wife. I wanted to support my husband. I understood his pain. It was important for me to recognize and validate his suffering and disappointment. But how much was I supposed to put his needs before my own?

It's not always easy, as a married couple, to know whose needs should be met first. Ideally, you want to make decisions based on what is beneficial to you both. It's important to consider how everyone will be affected by changes. However, it's rarely possible to make all conditions equal. Few situations allow both partners to get everything they need at the moment.

Sometimes you must sacrifice your own wants for your partner. This is essential in marriage. It is one of the costly risks of the adventure. Two people cannot completely combine their lives without suffering losses on both sides. There will be times when you must put your own needs aside to fulfill the goals and dreams of your partner. The key to this is balance. It should not always be one-sided. It's important to communicate openly and honestly with your spouse. Erv knew I didn't want to move. He knew I loved my job and was making progress on my Master's degree. He was not insensitive to my needs. However, he also felt the burden of being the primary wage earner in our family. He knew I wanted to stay home with our children, and I was pregnant. He was choosing to own the responsibility of being a husband and a father. It was not an easy path for him to follow but he asked me to support him, even though it was tough for me.

There is give and take in a healthy marriage. I make sacrifices for Erv. He makes sacrifices for me. We don't keep score of who has given up more. We have both experienced losses and they have been significant. They have also been rewarding. Supporting your spouse as they pursue a dream is a precious and life-giving gift. Your spouse needs to know you are on his side. She needs to be able to count on your support.

When we're dating, we are willing to make so many sacrifices to please our new partner. We go out of our way on a regular basis to make them happy. We should not stop when we get married. We must be willing to be uncomfortable in pursuit of unity with our spouse.

In an effort to support my husband, I willingly moved to Albany. We had no jobs waiting for us. No apartment to live in. No church to attend. We simply picked up and left. We moved all of our belongings into Erv's mother's abandoned beauty shop. Erv got a job working with a temp agency in Albany. I continued to commute two hours to Oneonta each week, staying with a generous family from church. We stayed in Albany with Erv's mother on the weekends.

As I finished out the school year, my pregnancy started to show. Reminded of our recent loss, I chose to thank God for this baby. I felt defeated and lost, but I refused to let our circumstances steal my joy. I had Erv and a new life within me. I had my in-laws and a few close friends. I would choose thankfulness and look forward to the future.

By the end of the school year, we managed to find a small basement apartment in downtown Troy. Our bedroom had no door and our soon-to-be baby's room was no bigger than a walk-in closet. The living room was so tiny we had to borrow a love seat from Erv's stepfather because our full-sized couch simply would not fit. He also contributed our first television—a used model with a 12 inch screen. Each night around 11 p.m., we would hear jingly songs from an ice cream truck out our back window. We were sure they were selling something other than ice cream at that hour of the night. The police frequented our neighborhood, and a drug house was shut down just a block from our apartment. This was not the dream environment I wanted for our new baby, but it was affordable and it was home.

Now that my migrant teaching job had come to an end, we brainstormed ways to continue paying our bills as well as saving for the future. Our budget remained stripped down to bare bones with no car payments, no cable bill, and no student loans. With Erv going back to graduate school, we would need another source of income. With my love for children and Erv's heart for entrepreneurship, we decided I should start my own home day care. I filed the necessary paperwork with the county and put up posters at the local grocery store. Within weeks I had my first customer—a single mother of two who worked full-time at the hospital across the street.

ERV'S TAKE

One of the best ways to address tight finances is to find creative ways to earn more money. We can become too focused on saving and cutting costs, when the real opportunity resides in our ability to earn more (either now or down the road). Investing in yourself, through education or experience, can pay more long-term dividends that budgeting and cost-cutting can ever achieve. Continue to learn and grow, making yourself more valuable for the future. Investing in yourself is one of the best investments you can ever make.

Since our apartment was so small, two children were all I could appropriately care for. A pair of young brothers would be deposited at my door at 7am each morning. Erv would head out to work in our only car. I'd put the 9-month-old in his stroller while taking the 4-year-old by the hand. We'd walk the four blocks up to the local park, singing along the way. The last block was all up-hill. My four-year-old friend would help me push his brother as I strained to get the stroller and my pregnant self up to the top. We'd spend a few hours at the park, and then head back to the apartment. After lunch, I'd put the boys napping in the living room while I rested on my bed. When we woke up, we had snack time, craft time, and playtime. Their mom would pick them up just before dinner, and I would be completely exhausted.

Erv would come home from his temp job tired and frustrated. He'd spend most days writing names on files, alphabetizing folders, and performing other tasks requiring less than a high school education. He found the work so demeaning and mindless he wanted to "stick pencils in his eyes." Surely a college degree should be able to land him a better job than this! We'd watch an hour or two of television after dinner, and then Erv would get some sleep before heading to his night job loading trucks at UPS. Working from 11 p.m. to 3 a.m. disrupted his sleep pattern, but this was the only part-time job he could find providing health benefits for our growing family and fitting around his 9 a.m. - 5 p.m. schedule.

My young husband was in a downward spiral. Between the lack of sleep and frustrating job circumstances, he would unexpectedly burst into fits of anger. One day he punched a hole in our living room wall. Another day he dented our kitchen wall. I was especially scared when he became so angry he punched the windshield of our car. The impact of his wedding ring caused the whole window to crack. I sat pregnant in the passenger seat, staring at the cracked windshield in front of me. I wanted to run. I wanted to get out of the car, pack all my stuff, and move home with my mom. The only thing that stopped me was the knowledge that I would eventually forgive him, and my mom might not.

Forgiveness is the most precious gift we can give our spouse. We all make mistakes. We all become frustrated. We all say and do things we do not mean. Forgiveness is not deserved or earned.

It is freely given. It is essential for every marriage.

Erv was not trying to harm or scare me. He would never hurt me. He would never intentionally put me in danger. He is my strongest advocate and greatest protector. He is not characterized by violence. He was frustrated and felt trapped by the unexpected circumstances of our life together. He was angry and made a mistake. But it still freaked me out.

When we reached home after the cracked windshield incident, I called a friend from Oneonta. A dear family from church had adopted us as their children. I spoke to our "dad" and told him what happened. He talked with Erv and helped us both get some perspective. He prayed with Erv, helping him to take a long-term view of our life and all God had already done. I was grateful for his support.

When you face a challenge like this in your marriage, seek some help. It's too difficult to navigate every trial alone. You need people you trust to confide in. Ideally, don't go behind your spouse's back. Involve them in the process as much as possible. You both need help. Be intentional about building relationships with other adults you can talk to.

Seek out another couple to serve as mentors. Is there someone at church, work, or in your community you admire? Do they have a healthy marriage? Invite them over for dinner. It doesn't have to be fancy—order a pizza if you want. Keep it simple, but make it happen. It is so helpful to have another couple's perspective. You don't need to be in a crisis to start a mentoring relationship.

After talking to our friend on the phone, Erv came to bed apologizing for what had happened. He asked me for forgiveness, and I granted it, as I knew I would. God had taken away my fear and filled my heart with hope. I knew that He did not give us this baby to cause us further suffering. I was convinced this expected child was a sign of better days to come. I would not allow our present struggles to cloud my hope in God's love for us.

I shared this with Erv as we lay in bed talking for what seemed like hours. We had committed long ago to, "not let the sun go down while we are still angry," as taught in Ephesians 4:26. With the baby's birth looming near, our conversation turned to a recurring theme: baby names. We had made some progress selecting names. This was an important decision to us. We believe the naming of a child is an opportunity to wish character upon them. If it was a boy, we would name him Brandon, meaning "brave prince." His middle name would be Christopher, after our campus minister, whom we both loved and admired. If it was a girl her name would be Mikayla, meaning "one who is like God." Our struggle was choosing a girl's middle name. I longed to name her after my beloved grandmother Marjorie, but I didn't like the possibility of my daughter being called, "Large Marge."

After reflecting on the encouragement God had provided me earlier in the night, I suggested we use the middle name Hope. She would always remind us to keep our hope in God strong despite our circumstances. Erv loved this idea. I was touched when he told me that naming her Hope would be like naming her after me since I am always full of hope. We wanted our child to have a strong faith in God to sustain him or her through any challenges he or she might one-day face. The name Hope would be a constant mark of that faith. After a trying evening and a long discussion, we slept peacefully in each other's arms, thankful to have renewed hope.

The next several weeks turned to more joyful times. Erv started his MBA and had a vision for a new career. We experienced the generosity of friends and family once again as they blessed us with baby showers. We received a car seat, stroller, high chair, and baby swing. Erv's mom found us a great crib at a garage sale. Erv's father crafted a beautiful hand-made cradle, adorned with stars. My college roommate sewed beautiful, Noah's Ark themed bedding and matching decorations for the walls. Family members and friends gave us a used playpen, baby clothes, bottles, and baby gates. As much as people told us that babies were expensive, we found that preparing for our first child came at little financial cost if we were willing to accept less than perfect hand-me-downs. We were quite sure the baby would not mind.

ERV'S TAKE

It took me time to learn an important life lesson. The current situation you face today is likely to look much different 12 months from now. This common reality has helped me to better cope with more difficult situations. There are seasons of life that are difficult, frustrating, painful, and dark. They are not our final destination. We get to move on from these seasons. God offers to walk with us through them and provides hope for a new future/life.

My first contractions arrived right on my due date. They came slowly at first, then faster and faster. I alerted my mom, and she quickly came to town. Once she arrived, the contractions slowed down. I consulted my midwife, and she concluded that it was either very early labor or false labor. To keep ourselves distracted, we decided to enjoy one of our favorite fall activities, picking apples. We headed up to the local orchard with my mom, timing the contractions as we drove. She was shocked to see me climbing trees while nine months pregnant, in the early stages of labor. Erv and I were hopeful the activity would move things along. Talk about an adventure! Too bad I can't say our first child was born in an apple tree.

By early evening, things were indeed moving along. I sent Erv to bed to get some rest before what I expected to be a very long night. My mom and I watched television and played cards to help pass time. When the contractions got stronger, I stopped playing and mom would hold my hand while I used my breathing exercises to manage the pain. At 1 a.m., when the pain became severe and the contractions were only five minutes apart, I woke Erv.

We hopped in the car and headed to the hospital, or so I thought. I was lying in the back seat, in terrible pain. After only two minutes, the car came to a stop. I was annoyed when I looked up and saw we were at a gas station. All day long I had asked Erv to stop and buy gas. We knew I was in labor and would need to go to the hospital sometime that day. The car was on E and the hospital was a 20 minute drive away. Now we were in downtown Troy at 1 a.m. where the only people around were the gas station attendant, a prostitute, and her next potential customer.

We got back on the road and traveled for about 15 minutes. I had resumed my horizontal position in the back seat, yet my partially obscured view revealed that we still were not headed to the hospital. I sat up awkwardly and asked, "Where are you going?!" Erv blushed and confessed that he had gone into "auto-pilot" and driven to his night job at UPS. I replied, "They do deliver, but not babies!"

We made a U-turn in the middle of the highway, my poor mom following behind us, not having a clue what was happening. She'd already followed us to the gas station and halfway to UPS. I was glad she hadn't given up and gone home! We finally arrived at the hospital and waited several more hours before the baby was ready to be born. I have never been so thankful to have Erv as my partner. He was by my side through every contraction, walking up and down the hospital corridors. Erv held my hand, read me Scripture, and prayed for me through the night and into the next day. At 5:38 p.m., Mikayla Hope Starr was finally born.

She has been filling us with hope ever since.

PART THREE

THE PARENTING JOURNEY

CHAPTER THIRTEEN

DO KIDS END THE ADVENTURE?

Some couples postpone having children as long as possible after they're married. We were planning to be one of those couples.

When you delay adding children to your family, you give yourself more time together exclusively as a couple. This can be a valuable season to establish healthy patterns of communication. Without a little one interrupting, you can enjoy long, in-depth conversations. You can stay up late or wake up early together, depending on your work schedules. You only have two people to coordinate around, so it's easier to find time to talk one-on-one. You can also date without a babysitter and discuss important issues when they arise.

Before you have children, you have fewer expenses. This allows you to spend less and establish a healthy habit of saving and investing. Ideally, both partners are able to work, contributing steadily to the family income. Once children arrive, childcare becomes a significant investment. Whether one parent chooses to stay home or you elect to pay for professional care, it can be costly.

Having a season of time for just the two of you also allows plenty of opportunities and freedom to enjoy one another sexually. Without another set of eyes around the house, you can indulge in physical intimacy anytime, anywhere. This generous amount of freedom is helpful in establishing a sense of comfort and safety in your sex life. It also allows for creativity and spontaneity.

However, having children is no excuse to neglect healthy communication, fiscal responsibility, and physical intimacy. All three need to remain a priority throughout your relationship. But there is no denying parenthood is a significant challenge to your communication, your finances, and your sex life.

Having time before children to establish these healthy habits is beneficial—but not all couples will have the luxury of waiting to have children. You may become pregnant right away or inherit children from a previous relationship. Regardless of when (or if) you begin a family, don't allow children (or any other excuse) to compromise your commitment to your marriage. The bond between you and your spouse comes first. A healthy, romantic relationship between parents contributes significantly to the emotional security of children.

We became parents much sooner than we planned. We had just over two years of alone time before we grew to be a family of three. Our pre-baby stage was a helpful time of discovering who we were as a couple. But, from the time Mikayla was born, we decided we wouldn't let being parents end our pursuit of excitement. We discovered parenthood added a whole new level of adventure to our relationship.

For me, the adventure began the moment they laid newborn

Mikayla in my arms. She pooped all over me. Not just ordinary poop. A baby's first poop is black and tar-like. It's basically the most disgusting kind of poop on earth. I had just survived 21 hours of labor, and I was covered with "first poop." This was my welcome to motherhood. I didn't even care. Mikayla was the most beautiful thing I had ever seen.

I was honestly a little surprised. I didn't assume Erv and I would make ugly babies. I had simply been conditioned to expect a less-than-perfect baby. When we went through childbirth classes, they showed us picture after picture of scary looking babies. We were instructed not to expect a beautiful baby. Being a self-proclaimed good listener, I was prepared to meet a cone-head, prune-faced, hairy baby. Instead, my baby had a perfectly round head, the slightest bit of light brown hair, big blue eyes, and a perfect little smile. Yes, Mikayla was born smiling. Some say it was gas, but it most definitely was not. Maybe.

As the nurses struggled to scrape the poop off my stomach, I looked down at her perfect little face. "It's you. You're finally here." The moment I spoke, she turned her little head and looked right at me. It's a moment I will never forget. She knew me. She recognized my voice. It was awesome!

I held her through the night. I held her through the next day. By the second night, the nurses insisted I send her to the nursery for a little while so I could rest. I lay alone in my hospital bed thinking about her. Those perfect little fingers. Those big blue eyes. Her precious smile. An hour later, I asked them to bring her back to me. I missed her.

I always knew my mother loved me. She told me almost every day my whole life. She had this little joke. She'd say, "Remember, I don't like you. I love you." She would write this to me in birthday cards and whisper it in my ear before I went to sleep at night. She showed me her love in action. She drove me to school because I hated taking the bus. She made me lunch because I hated buying it at school. She sat on the side of my bed when I was sick. She read me stories and put a bendy straw in my Coke so I could sip it lying down.

I was spoiled. Not with possessions. Those were quite limited. I was spoiled with love. It was an unconditional love that seemed to have no end. Now, as a mother myself, I realized just how loved I was. I was crazy in love with Mikayla. I would do anything for her and I had known her for only two days. How much more did my mom love me? She had loved me for 24 years. The thought overwhelmed me.

My mom stayed with us for the first two weeks after Mikayla came home from the hospital. She was very helpful, and I was extremely grateful. The adjustment to parenthood was a bit awkward for us. It was actually easier for Erv. Being the oldest of four siblings, he had cared for younger children most of his life. His brother Adam is 16 years younger. Erv had changed diapers, given baths, and was very comfortable around babies. I loved children but had never taken care of a newborn. Mikayla seemed so tiny and fragile to me.

I remember calling the pediatrician to make Mikayla's first doctor's appointment. "Yes, I need to make an appointment for my (choke, pause) daughter." The word felt so foreign coming out of my mouth. I was the daughter, not the mother. Erv and I both felt like we were babysitting someone else's child. At 24, neither of us felt old enough to be legitimate parents. We kept expecting Mikayla's real parents to show up any minute, ready to take her home. After about two weeks, the reality set in. No one was coming to pick her up. This kid was here to stay.

During our pre-marital counseling, we had been told having a baby did not make you a family. We were taught that as soon as you were married, you were a family. Children would be welcome additions to your existing family. We wanted to love our baby and give her everything she needed, but we did not want to neglect our relationship with each other.

We had seen this misstep in other marriages, and we were determined to avoid it. This, however, is easier said than done. When you have a child, they easily become the center of your world. A screaming baby is hard to ignore. A screaming spouse is easy to walk away from. Babies are so sweet and adorable. You long to make them the center of your attention. Their needs are ever-present and it is demanding. If you are not intentional about sharing that focus with your spouse, you can unexpectedly grow apart.

It takes a while to get the hang of this, but persist in making your spouse a priority from day one. With each of our children, Erv and I were determined to go out on a date within the first week after the baby was born. On our first post-baby date, we literally went to a coffee shop about one mile away from our house for less than an hour. You will be nervous leaving your newborn baby. You might be nursing and need to come home in a short amount of time. Regardless, you need to start a healthy habit of dating from the beginning of your life together as parents. Go on a date as soon as you can. Seriously. Get out there!

We know many couples who go months or even years without dating after they have children. They simply can't seem to find the time. If you want your marriage to last, you will need to make the time. You and your spouse will be together long after your children are grown and gone. You need to continually invest in your marriage, beginning when your children are babies. Don't miss out on eighteen years of enjoying each other.

Another way to invest in your marriage while parenting is to include your children in your adventures! Your entire world does not need to revolve around your baby and their schedule. A healthy pattern of eating and sleeping is important for your baby. Establishing a routine is beneficial to their growth and development. However, as much as possible, this schedule should be developed in harmony with your family needs.

For us, this meant including our children in our active, adventurous lifestyle. We brought Mikayla on walks, hikes, and bike rides. We took her to movies, plays, and parties. Once, we put her to sleep in a bedroom at Erv's brother's Super Bowl party with a rowdy crowd cheering in the living room next door. She was so accustomed to this practice of falling asleep in a strange, noisy place she slept right through the whole party. We were (and still are) always on the go and Mikayla simply went along with us.

We also made sure to reserve consistent time for just the two of us. Living near family was especially helpful. Grandparents, aunts, and uncles were so anxious to spend time with Mikayla, they practically shoved us out the door to go on dates. This was a blessing! Don't deny the grandparents' wishes to spend time with the kids. This is a great opportunity for you to enjoy time together.

Even when family wasn't available, I found childcare exchange with other young moms was easy and helpful. I would watch a friend's child one day, and she would watch mine the next. We didn't pay for babysitting the first six years of Mikayla's life! You can do this as well. Don't allow the expense of babysitting or the inconvenience of making extra arrangements to be a hindrance to dating. Ask friends and family to help. Take turns with friends who also have children. Put initiative into your dating life. It will pay big dividends in your marriage.

There are many ways to keep the weekly dates themselves inexpensive. We frequently enjoyed walks in Frear Park, the dollar movie theatre (a fantastic Albany find!), and Cracker Barrel. It was during this stage of our marriage that Cracker Barrel became my favorite restaurant. Here was our Cracker Barrel strategy. We would put our name on the list to be seated and browse in the gift shop while we waited. We wouldn't buy anything, but I'd get cool ideas of craft stuff I could make for Christmas and birthday presents. Once seated, we would order dessert or hot drinks. If you like the atmosphere of eating out (which we did since we lived in a tiny basement apartment), getting dessert or coffee instead of dinner still gets you out to a nice place but cuts your bill significantly. For us, it was less about the food and more about the experience. After dessert, we would sit in front of the fireplace on the stone hearth and play checkers. We would casually chat by the crackling fire, acting as if this was our very own living room. It was a wonderful place of escape and enjoyment—a favorite date for about $5.

Bring your children into your marriage adventure. They are a welcome part of the family. But, remember your first love, the one you chose to spend your life with. The best gift you can give your children is not something purchased but the gift of a loving relationship between you and your spouse. Assuring them that you love each other will create a great sense of security and belonging that will propel them into their future. Let your kids know that you value each other and prioritize your relationship and watch how strong and confident it makes them.

You don't have to spend a lot of money on your children. We didn't pay to feed Mikayla for months. Please don't call Child Protective Services—I was simply committed to nursing my baby and successfully did so for six months. I realize that it is not for everyone. It, however, is excellent food for the baby, helps you get back into shape, and is totally and completely free. Formula, on the other hand, is expensive—that is why they give it to you for free at the hospital! During the first three weeks of nursing, I was tempted to give it up many times—usually in the middle of the night when Erv was peacefully sleeping. The free can of formula would call to me from the cupboard, "C-a-r-r-i-e! I'm here w-a-i-t-i-n-g. You know you want to come o-p-e-n me and let Erv feed the b-a-b-y!"

ERV'S TAKE

Nature can provide in ways a store cannot. Sometimes we are persuaded to buy into more costly ideas (formula, name brand clothes and groceries, tourist settings) where we have other options. You can enjoy time together for little to no cost. The real test of the value is not the price tag, but the memories created and feelings and experiences shared.

The same temptation came with disposable diapers. They send these home from the hospital with you for free too. There were many days when I was on my knees, swishing a poopy cloth diaper out in the toilet, that I would imagine myself simply tossing a neat, tidy disposable diaper into the trash can. These were the moments when I would train my mind to move from this image to a picture of myself at the grocery store checkout, paying $20 a week for diapers that would end up sitting in a landfill until Mikayla went off to college 18 years later. I stuck to the cloth diapers.

The cloth diaper commitment required additional resolve since we did not own a dryer. Erv's mother and stepfather had given us a washing machine for Christmas, but we couldn't afford a dryer. In many ways this was a blessing. We did a fair amount of laundry, and the cost of running the dryer would have added up quickly as well. We had three collapsible dryer racks instead. These would be lined up side-by-side in our living room, each one full of white, cloth rectangles. Given the size of our tiny living room, the space was literally wall-to-wall diapers twice a week.

When Mikayla started eating solid food, we once again found old-fashioned ideas to be most economical. Instead of buying jars of baby food, I would cook simple ingredients like carrots, apples, broccoli, etc. Once the item was cooked, I would put it in the blender with a little water until it had the consistency of baby food. Next, I would spoon the mushy food into ice cube trays, cover them with plastic wrap, and place the trays in the freezer. When it was time to eat, I would pop out a single cube of the food I wanted and heat it up. As Mikayla's appetite grew, I took out more cubes. By the time Mikayla was old enough to start eating table food, I purchased a simple food processor (that you crank by hand) at a garage sale for $5. When we ate our meals, I would put some of whatever food we were eating into the processor. Erv and I would take turns mixing Mikayla's food. This also helped Mikayla become accustomed to the taste of the food our family typically eats. We were committed early on to help our children not be picky eaters. Since most child-friendly convenience foods are pre-packaged, unhealthy, and expensive, we wanted to avoid them.

In general, we found that going ahead and "sweating the small stuff" saved us money every time. When we went out for the day as a family, we would pack our own food, avoiding the high priced food at concession stands and fast food joints. We frequently carried water bottles to avoid buying drinks on the run. Erv packed peanut butter and jelly sandwiches for work every day. When he came home, I would rinse out the plastic baggie and use it again. We found that buying the store brand was almost always as good as the name brand. If we preferred a name brand, we'd use a coupon or wait for it to go on sale and stock up. We bought things in bulk and divided them up into reused canning jars to keep them fresh. I lined up these jars on my counter, finding the variety of textures and colors to make an attractive display.

ERV'S TAKE

Okay, even I think we are crazy, or at least a little over-zealous. So maybe you don't want to re-wash plastic bags (even if it is good for the environment and wallet). You can still see the value of small steps taken over a period of time. Setting good habits re-garding small decisions does add up. It also is good preparation for the time of life when you have more. More money, things, opportunities, people to care for…practice with the small; succeed with the big. The idea of tipping points comes to mind. At some point you add just enough weight to one side of the scale to begin to shift the weight on the other side. As you make wise financial decisions, they begin to add up. Eventually, they shift the weight of your financial situation as the combined impact frees you in new ways.

We found this stage of being poor to be the best time to have a baby. When it came to clothes and toys, if she didn't have the very best, she didn't know what she was missing. Her very first Christmas, we didn't buy her a single present. It wasn't because we didn't love her, but because it seemed a waste of money. At two months old, she certainly didn't feel she was being robbed of the perfect Christmas. If we saved that money, it would be worth more when she was older and actually cared. Just having a baby with us for the first time at Christmas was a priceless gift.

Creative problem solving as a couple really strengthened our marriage. Because we functioned as a team on these cost saving strategies, it built a great bond between us. Finding inexpensive ways to raise our child became a common goal. In some ways, it was a bit of a game. How cheap could we be and still have a happy, healthy child? It turns out, pretty darn cheap!

Parenting on a budget is a great time for team building. See each other as your greatest asset. Share your cost-cutting ideas and support one another's initiative. It's easy to criticize an idea when it isn't ours. We immediately see the flaws in our spouse's strategy and believe we could come up with something far superior. This does not help your relationship. Look for the good in your partner's idea. If it has merit, support it. When it succeeds, celebrate it. When it fails, learn from it and avoid saying, "I told you so."

CHAPTER FOURTEEN

INVEST IN YOURSELF

A successful marriage is made of two whole individuals. When you grow and develop as a person, you strengthen your marriage.

When you're first married, you become easily wrapped up in your spouse. It's tempting to orient your entire world around your partner. Once you have children, they typically become the center of your attention. In the midst of these new relationships, it's easy to neglect yourself. This is a mistake.

Both your spouse and your children need you as a whole and growing person. It's not selfish or neglectful to grow your skills, pursue your interests, and develop relationships outside of your home. It's certainly possible to take these choices to an extreme and abandon your marriage or family, but this is a rare occurrence. When you have open, honest communication with your spouse about your needs and interests, you will commonly find ways to accommodate growth in both of you.

I'm thankful Erv supports my personal development. He has always believed in my strengths and gifts, and encouraged me to pursue my interests. Likewise, I have done the same for him. It is not always easy, and we have both had seasons where we had to put our own desires on hold to support the other. It's easier to be patient and understanding during these times when you know your turn is coming. If you establish a pattern of supporting each other early on, you will have security during the times when you are the one making sacrifices.

Because our careers were not turning out as we expected right after college, Erv and I both pursued some surprising pathways. We were both stretched and grown in unforeseen ways.

Always on the lookout for new opportunities, Erv found a company promising big commissions for part-time work. He went through the interview process, a rigorous training program, and finally purchased his demonstration products. Similar to our first business venture, Erv was booking appointments with friends and family, this time trying to sell them high-priced knives. He worked hard at it, looking for the promised big pay-out equaling his effort.

He also went back to school. Erv decided to invest in his future by starting his MBA. He worked his traditional job all day, attended classes in the evening, and made sales calls on the weekend. He was driven to make our situation better for himself and our family. We both made sacrifices in pursuit of what we hoped would be future success.

After months of juggling work, school, and his new business, we came to the conclusion that there is no such thing as, "get rich quick." Disciplined effort to make tough choices over and over again is what would eventually move us from our current situation to a place of financial stability. We reminded ourselves that each dollar we saved today would be invested and multiplied in our future.

ERV'S TAKE

For a few, financial success will come quickly. The majority of us will not develop the next iPhone or win the lottery. For us, we build wealth over time. We build financial stability by making sacrifices today in the immediate for tomorrow and the distant future. We say "no" to our current self, to bless our future selves. But this too can be taken too far. As one who is prone to think about tomorrow, we don't want to lose the preciousness of today, for this is the time we are guaranteed. Use this time well, love fully, and embrace the moments. Still, the ant gathers in the summer to be ready for the winter. We learn to balance today and tomorrow in our financial decisions.

It was at this time of financial struggle when we started a retirement account. Investing in your retirement in your mid-20s allows your account to double many more times as opposed to waiting until you are financially comfortable in your 30s or 40s. We didn't wait until we had "extra" money to invest. We made sacrifices and started investing in our future as soon as possible. We didn't want the pressing needs of today to overshadow our long-term plans.

ERV'S TAKE

The reality of compounding interest is that time is on your side. The earlier you put money away, the more valuable it becomes when you are older. It made me sad one day to realize it would take decades to save a million dollars (still in process). Then I realized that if I received average stock market returns, it would only take several years to earn the second million. Oh, how I wished I could just start at the one million mark! Unfortunately, I can't. However, I did put a little away in my 20's, which could turn thousands into millions in a normal lifetime.

I think investing in your spouse works similarly. You can make small deposits in your spouse's emotional bank account (words of affirmation, loving gifts, acts of service, a loving touch, a listening ear, support for a dream). These little investments will add up over time. The earlier you start making them, the greater return you will see from them.

Education was another strategic investment we made in ourselves. Committed to avoiding debt, pursuing a Master's degree was a calculated risk. We knew attaining advanced degrees would open doors of opportunity for us. Up to this point, we had paid for all of our graduate courses with cash. By the end of Erv's first semester working on his MBA, he got an idea. While looking at the course catalog, he realized that the only difference in coursework for an MBA and PhD was a little thing called a "dissertation." "How hard could that be?" Erv surmised. He immediately applied for a doctorate program in Organizational Management.

Excited about this new course of action, Erv anxiously awaited the results of his application. He studied up on the program, discovering he would learn about managing not only for-profit businesses but also public and non-profit organizations. This was a perfect fit as yet another door of opportunity opened.

In less than one year, his temp job writing names on file folders had evolved into the Accounts Receivable Manager position for a small, local company. Erv was pleased with the promotion but was dissatisfied with receiving temp worker pay for a job with significant responsibility. He requested a raise but was told the company couldn't afford to pay him more.

Always on the lookout for other options, Erv had taken a Civil Service exam months earlier. He performed well on the test and was offered a position in county government. When he tendered his resignation at his current job, they offered him a raise. Erv was not impressed by their lack of integrity, suddenly having the money to give him a raise. (This company incidentally went out of business a few years later due to fraud.)

As Erv got accustomed to his new job at the county, I was struggling with mine. Many women find caring for small children while raising their own to be rewarding and convenient. Now that Mikayla had arrived, this was not my experience.

With three small children in my care, our tiny apartment was extremely crowded. Between the dryer racks, playpens, and high chairs, we could barely move from room to room. Naptime was nothing short of a disaster. As soon as I would get one baby to sleep, the other would cry, and wake the first one up. I'd get both babies to sleep, and the 4 year old would start singing or throw a toy into his brother's crib. And there was no escaping the house.

The winter snow piled high on the un-shoveled city sidewalks, making them impassible with the stroller. Driving was not an option since Erv was gone at work with the only car. I tried bundling up all three children for a walk to the park. I carried one baby in the backpack, the other in the front pack, and the four-year-old walked along by my side. Carrying two babies in full snow suits while tromping through a foot of snow across four city blocks is not easy.

By the time I got to the top of the final hill, I was covered with sweat. We reached the park and the four-year-old took off running. I chased after him, babies bouncing in front of and behind me. Mikayla started crying, and I collapsed on a park bench. I yelled for my four-year-old friend to come to me, "NOW!"

Thankfully, he obeyed.

Baby Mikayla was hungry. While I was committed to nursing, this was not a convenient time or place to get this done. I was sitting on the bench with a fidgety preschooler on one side of me and a propped-up toddler on the other. Trying to feed Mikayla discreetly through three layers of winter clothing while managing to stay warm and modest was an accomplishment.

Fortunately, both boys stayed still until Mikayla was finished and I could get up from the bench and push all three of them on the miniature child-safe swings. The winter wind seemed to cut right through my clothing. Not wanting to be responsible for another woman's children getting frostbite, I packed the kids up, and we walked back through the snow to the apartment. That was the last day I ventured outside with the children all winter. I had been scarred for life. Or at least, for winter.

Being a new mom can be tough. Whether you are a full-time stay-at-home mom or you're a working mother, it's an adjustment. When the childcare business became difficult, I felt lost and without options. I knew I wanted to care for my child and yet I wanted to contribute to our family income. Erv was working diligently all the time. I wanted to do my part but I wanted to do something rewarding. Neither of us would be satisfied by simply making money.

I loved being a teacher, but I didn't want to return to a job taking me away from our new baby all day long. For many mothers, this is their best and preferred option. I know many women who are devoted mothers and work full-time outside of their home. I admire and appreciate these women. They use their gifts and talents to support their families. When they come home from work, the work does not stop. They care for the children and husbands even when they're exhausted. It's amazing.

It wasn't for me. I was willing to work, but I wanted a different solution. I was determined to find a way to be a full-time parent and a part-time worker. Surely there was a creative option where I could do both.

By spring, I closed my childcare business. Erv and I had begun volunteering with the youth ministry at our new church, and I loved it. Working with teenagers was the highlight of my week. I longed to do something of eternal value that also allowed me to be a full-time parent. I applied for a job with Campus Ambassadors, the same organization that had been so instrumental to building our faith while in college.

I was overjoyed to be appointed as a campus minister in May! I would be starting a new ministry at the University at Albany. This was scary and intimidating, but I was up for the challenge.

In the meantime, Erv got less exciting news from the same university. They denied his application for the PhD program. He had excellent grades, GMAT scores, and references. The problem was his essay. Always frank about his feelings, Erv had shared his career goals were to become a small business owner and a college professor. They wanted to see greater passion for research. He had none. Erv was discouraged at this rejection.

I remember bringing him the letter during his lunch break at work. Erv had given me the car for the day so I could grocery shop. I stopped by his office on the way home from the store. We sat in the parking lot on the hood of the car, enjoying the warm spring day while Mikayla napped peacefully in her car seat.

It's so important to capture moments like this. You need to create opportunities to enjoy and appreciate one another. It would have been easy to simply drive home, put Mikayla down in her crib and unload the groceries. It's so natural to become wrapped up in your own list of tasks, overlooking your spouse. We typically think of ways our spouse could be helping us instead of discovering how we might support them.

I knew Erv would need my support. This was going to be a difficult blow and I wasn't sure how he'd handle it. Rejection is a terrible emotion. It was important for Erv to know I believed in him. Putting my own schedule aside to make him a priority was an investment in our marriage.

It was such a pleasant moment relaxing there in the afternoon sun, I hated to ruin it with the letter, but I had no choice. I am terrible at pretending, and Erv knew something was up. I gave him the letter so he could read it for himself. He was angry and disappointed. Fortunately, we were in a public place so he maintained some pretty good self-control. We talked for a while, and then Erv headed back in to work. I drove home crying tears of disappointment for him.

One of my husband's greatest strengths is he does not take "no" for an answer. Refusing to give up, he stayed in the MBA program, carefully selecting courses that would fulfill the MBA or the PhD. He would reapply to the PhD program in the fall after making strategic connections in the department. He would also rewrite his essay to show greater interest in research.

After a few months working in the Department for Youth at the county, a position opened up in the Department of Economic Development. This position was intriguing to Erv. It would allow him to see the whole process of starting a new business from a different vantage point. He would also learn about government planning and the establishment of roads, buildings, and neighborhoods. He admired the director of this department as a person of character and integrity, knowing he could learn a lot from him. Erv was chosen for the position, and we celebrated the new job—and the raise that came along with it.

We approached our second year in Albany excited about these opportunities. We both had new careers, our baby was healthy and growing, and our savings was finally starting to accumulate. We felt a sense of progress and achievement. As we celebrated Mikayla's first birthday, I realized I needed to talk to Erv about something important, preferably in public.

CHAPTER FIFTEEN

HOW TO GIVE BAD NEWS TO A GOOD SPOUSE

The longer you're married, the more you learn about your spouse. This seems pretty obvious. The challenge is to adapt and adjust in response to what you learn. It's easy to simply do things the way you've always done them, or want to do them, regardless of what works for your spouse. This is a bad idea. Your ever-growing storehouse of knowledge about your partner can be used to bless your spouse and maybe even make your life more pleasant at the same time. The choice is yours to make…do what comes naturally, or be wise and adjust accordingly.

When I have news, my instinct is to blurt it out as soon as possible. If you have news you want shared with as many people as possible, just tell me. I'm happy to tell the world on your behalf. If you have a secret that you don't want leaked until a very special time to a very special person, please don't tell me without first saying, "This is a secret." I'm happy to find out when it becomes public knowledge. I'm not saying that I am in the habit of betraying confidences. In fact, I'm capable of keeping others' secrets and have several that I refuse to tell. It's just my natural inclination to share news. I'm a sharer. That's who I am.

This is especially true when it comes to my own news. When it's my birthday, I tell everyone. The mailman. The teller at the bank. The grocery store clerk. Basically, anyone willing to listen to me. When I landed my new job with Campus Ambassadors, I spent days on the phone sharing my joy. When I had my braces off, I sent pictures of my new-found teeth to everyone I knew. I enjoy writing those newsy Christmas letters telling all your friends and family everything you've done over the past year. I am an effervescent, good news sharer.

On a beautiful fall day in 1996, I had news to share. Good news to be celebrated with the world! But I knew better. I had been married to Erv for three years. We had been friends for twice that long. There is a time and place to share news with Erv. I cannot blurt out news when it first comes to me. I need to wait until he can hear about it, and I must think about how he will react. His reaction is somewhat within my control by my choosing where and how I tell him things. If I share news with Erv the moment he arrives home from work after a long, hard day, he will not receive it well. If I blurt out my excitement when he clearly has news of his own to share, then I steal his thunder. If he's tired, he will be sound asleep before I arrive at the climax of my story. I have learned to patiently wait to share my news until the perfect time when my husband can be as excited as I am.

I have also learned that good news to me is not always good news to Erv. Giving Erv news that he might think is bad can be complicated. When I think of times I have shared bad news with Erv, the phrase, "don't shoot the messenger," comes to mind. Anger can be an unpleasant reaction to bad news, and I have been the object of Erv's misplaced anger more than once. I avoid it whenever I can. Outbursts of anger are like landmines: I have learned to distinguish and carefully navigate around them. Sometimes, however, I have no choice but to head straight for them.

A landmine was inevitably in my path. I had potentially bad news for Erv. Our plans were finally falling into place but were about to get turned upside down again. He had just recently recovered from the rejection to the Ph.D. program. Was he ready to deal with another curveball? As I thought about delivering the rejection letter last spring, I realized an important lesson was learned that day. I brought it to him at lunch because I didn't want to wait until he came home. It wasn't a planned decision but an impulsive one.

His reaction taught me to be more strategic with my "news telling." Erv had demonstrated self-control in the face of rejection because we were in public. He didn't lose his temper with other people around. By the time he had come home and we were in private, he had had plenty of time to calm down and be rational about it. Since I knew I was likely to get a strong reaction to this latest piece of news, I decided to share it with him on the Campus Ambassadors fall retreat. We would be in a setting focused on our faith, and there would be lots of people around.

Is this what you do when you discover something new about your spouse? Do you stick to what comes naturally, or do you adjust and make the most of your newfound knowledge? Change is not easy. Our past experiences have a powerful influence over us. We can easily blame our personalities or our upbringing, emphatically stating, "This is just the way I am," instead of learning and growing along with our spouses. When we make excuses to not change, we are missing an opportunity to improve our marriage.

I wanted to blurt out my news. I wanted to tell Erv the instant I discovered it, but I knew better. I had learned valuable information about my husband and knew I needed to wait. For the sake of my marriage, I patiently kept the news to myself until the second day of the retreat.

We were standing just outside of the large meeting hall when I bravely stepped on to what I knew to be a landmine. "Do you remember when you were in school, and you would pick teams in gym class? Sometimes you were the captain and got to pick who was on your team. Other times, people were put on your team, and they were not your choice. You had to try your best to win the game with the team you were given."

This was my attempt at a "word picture," a technique taught to us by our small group leaders at church. It helps you communicate your feelings with your spouse. When you paint a mental picture for your partner, something they can relate to, it allows them to experience what you're feeling. This is especially helpful when you know your spouse may not feel the same way as you about a situation. You want to create a word picture eliciting an emotional reaction.

Sports analogies in general seemed to work well with Erv. They were a big part of his life and usually helped him relate. Too bad my experience with sports at the time was limited to gym class and one season keeping stats for the varsity boys' soccer team. I tried my best to paint my gym class picture. Erv was staring at me, confused. I decided to get to the point. "Well, God has given us another member for our team. We need to be thankful for him or her and make it work."

"Are you pregnant again?!" was his immediate and startled response.

"Um, yep," was my elegant-with-words-under-pressure reply.

We are clearly very good at getting pregnant. This was the third time in three years. I waited for the angry outburst. There was only silence. I longed for a happy, joyful reaction, but I was content. We were trying to get back on our five-year-plan. We had been thrown off course multiple times, but we were finally making what felt like forward progress. This was not part of the plan.

In the evening, I was shocked when he publicly shared our news with everyone on the Campus Ambassadors retreat! He asked for people to celebrate with us and keep us in their prayers. I thanked God for answering my prayers for a favorable reaction. Not only had Erv stayed calm, but he had acted in very "Carrie-like" fashion, sharing our news as soon as possible with everyone he could. It seemed he was learning about me as well. He knew this was happy news for me and I wanted to share it. By making this announcement, he made me feel incredibly loved.

When we returned home from the retreat, we received more good news. Erv was accepted into the Ph.D. program! His excellent performance on his MBA coursework, his networking with decision makers at the University, and an updated essay including research plans had changed people's minds, and now Erv was an official doctoral candidate. This would not be the last time we learned persistence pays off. Erv continued taking classes at the University at Albany in the evening, while working at the county during the day. I started working at the University at Albany two days and two evenings a week doing campus ministry, usually taking Mikayla with me. To keep from passing like ships in the night, Erv came home from work for lunch or met me on campus where we'd enjoy packed sandwiches and quality family time almost every day. We wanted to stay connected to each other while pursuing our new individual adventures.

It wasn't as easy as it sounds. It was inconvenient for Erv to come home for lunch. Some days he'd spend as much time in the car as he did at home. Our on-campus time was valuable. He could have spent those hours studying or grading papers. Yet, we didn't want to grow apart. With our busy schedules, it would have been easy for this to happen. We were both enjoying significant personal growth in our new careers. We were having unique experiences and meeting interesting people. It was an intentional choice to continuing pursuing each other.

When you begin a new personal adventure, it's very exciting. A new job or position fills you with energy and life. You can become consumed with the excitement of the moment and slowly give it more and more of your energy and attention. Maintaining your marriage can seem an unpleasant chore. Suddenly, your relationship, which was fresh and new, is now boring and routine. Neglecting your spouse in the face of a rewarding career is common. It's also an abandonment of your wedding vows.

When you marry, you promise to honor and cherish. This means making your partner a precious priority. Erv missed opportunities for advancement at work because he didn't work through his lunch hour. He also passed on social time with his fellow students who regularly went out together after class. He closed these doors to make time for our relationship. He chose to pursue the adventure of our marriage, even when fresh, new adventures presented themselves on a regular basis.

I faced similar temptations in my new job as well. I loved being on campus and was regularly asked to stay later with my students. They invited me out to coffee and over to their apartments for dinner. They had emergency situations needing attention and counsel. There was always more work to be done, more meetings to schedule, and more lessons to prepare. Because I'm a highly relational person, it was difficult to pull myself away from my students and focus on my marriage. Having those scheduled lunches and choosing to be home for dinner every night protected my first priority.

I was also trying to make my child a priority. Little Mikayla was a big hit on campus. I'd bring her in the baby backpack and stand it up on a table in the student union. I'd sit at the table and chat with students on their way to and from classes. She loved watching all the commotion, and the students absolutely adored her. Female students especially would stop in their tracks to comment on her big blue eyes. "Oh, my gosh! She is so beautiful!" was a common response as students spotted her on their way to lunch. She was a fantastic conversation starter.

I did have one skeptical student criticize me. He accused me of bringing my baby to campus just so people would talk to me. My calm response was, "Actually, I'm just cheap. I can't afford childcare, and I enjoy having her with me. How do you feel about working mothers?" This opened up a wonderful conversation with a total stranger about his close relationship with his working mom. He became a regular, stopping by my table to chat each week.

I never thought I'd like being a working mom. My dream was to stay home with my children as my own mom did. I was so thankful God had provided a way to do both. As Mikayla grew, I took her to campus in the stroller. I was given the kind you could adjust to recline, and she napped in the stroller while I taught afternoon Bible studies. When she started walking and running, my students enjoyed taking her for tours around campus and showing her off at their dorm rooms. Because I was able to take Mikayla to work with me, I was there for her first words, her first steps, and her first ice cream cone. These were precious moments I didn't want to miss. I know not all moms have the opportunity to do this, so I was especially thankful to be a full-time parent while pursuing a part-time career. While I didn't make a lot of money at this job, I was glad to be contributing something to our family income while raising our child and working a job I loved.

Erv was thankful for my contribution but still felt the stress of providing for our family while attending grad school and trying to save for a business. I could go back to teaching but that would mean paying for childcare. The increased earnings would be cancelled out by the childcare costs, purchasing work clothes, and other related expenses. I would also miss out on being with our babies. Erv could work a second job, but he was already too busy with work and grad school. I wanted our children to grow up knowing their father, and he was committed to being involved in their lives. This meant we needed to find another way to earn money that didn't require either of us working more. I thought it was impossible. My visionary husband thought differently.

ERV'S TAKE

It is said that necessity is the mother of invention. When you find yourself in challenging situations, you need to explore creative ideas and solutions. It can be exciting to explore ways to keep your priorities while achieving your dreams. It was the absence of money that forced us to consider a living situation that enabled our priorities and goals to be met simultaneously. Twenty years later we still use this solution, and our family's lives have been richly blessed by the relationships it has helped forge.

CHAPTER SIXTEEN

ROI, DIY, AND SEX

There are two primary ways to improve your financial situation as a couple: earning money and saving money. Erv had discovered a unique way for us to do both at the same time, although most couples aren't willing to do it.

The majority of married couples dream of owning a home. Home ownership has almost become a rite of passage signaling arrival at adulthood. We all assume we will eventually have a place to call our own. A mortgage is the ultimate mark of independence and success.

After three years of marriage, we had finally saved enough money for a meager down payment on an inexpensive house, but our home would not be the typical American dream home. Instead, we were looking for a multi-family house. This would allow us to build equity in a property but also collect rent from our tenants. It would also mean sharing our home with others. This was a sacrifice we were willing to make.

The timing was excellent. Our tiny basement apartment didn't have sufficient space to accommodate a second child. I was anxious to get away from the mice, roaches, and other critters sharing our home underground. It was time to move. We started looking at underpriced multi-family homes in need of repair.

The next several weeks involved searching home listings and driving all over God's creation with our real estate agent. The places we explored were either side-by-side duplexes, up-and-downstairs apartment houses, or multi-unit apartment houses. By purchasing one of these homes, we could live in our own unit and rent out the others, which would in turn help pay our mortgage. The more units the house had, the more income it could provide. Erv was in favor of a three-to-four family situation, maximizing our return on investment.

More units also meant more work finding renters, more upkeep on the property, and more possible problems. We looked at many, many properties, considering carefully what we wanted as a family as well as a good rental location. Erv kept a close eye on the numbers. The sale price itself was less a factor than its relationship to the rental income. We were searching for an affordable price where the rental income would cover the mortgage.

We decided to purchase a three-family home located on the east side of Troy. It had been on the market for more than a year, so the price was significantly discounted. This new home moved us out of the dangerous, high crime neighborhood in which we currently lived. It also gave us more room as a family. It was a large, green colonial with white shutters and a generous front porch—perfect for the wooden swing Erv made for me. There were two small apartments on the first floor and a large two-bedroom apartment on the second floor.

We excitedly moved in on the second floor. The house came with a double carport and a very small back yard for the kids.

Mikayla's bedroom was larger than her previous "closet-sized" room, which was perfect since she would soon be sharing with her younger sibling. We had been told our next baby was a girl, but were cautioned, "Don't paint." Two girls sharing a bedroom would be convenient. I was hopeful.

I was happy our new apartment had a dining room and a larger living room, and our bedroom actually had a door. With Mikayla growing, it was important for Erv and me to have privacy in our room. Even after we became parents, we kept our commitment to sleeping naked. Now Mikayla was over a year old, and she was more aware of her surroundings. We didn't want to scar our child by catching us without our pajamas on. Although we encourage creativity and spontaneity, we also believe it's important for sex to be sacred. Keep a lock on your bedroom door and save sex on the couch for the nights when the kids stay at Grandma's.

Your sex life can easily suffer once you become parents. Fear of children hearing or seeing is a valid concern. Playing music in your room or in theirs is a helpful distraction. Sometimes stealth mode can add to the fun. (I'm hearing the "Mission Impossible" theme song in my head right now.) If you want to fully enjoy one another sexually, you need to not be concerned about the kids. Keep them in their own room and teach them from a young age to respect your privacy. Our children know our bedroom is sacred ground. It's not a place where they assume they are welcome. They always knock and ask for permission before entering and they only do that if they need our attention immediately. Otherwise, they've been taught to not interrupt us while we're in our bedroom. This is beneficial to our marriage. Establish this guideline early.

Another hindrance to your sex life after children is fatigue. Children require energy. The workday doesn't end when you come home. By the time you finally have the children in bed, you or your spouse might feel too tired to exert more energy. Start a pattern of an early bedtime when your children are young. It may be difficult at first, but it will be worth it. When the children go to bed early, you have more alone time in the evening. If you are always pushing your time for intimacy later and later into the evening, you'll find yourself enjoying sex less and less. Sex is one of the greatest adventures of marriage. Don't allow parenting to sabotage this incredible gift from God.

You may not feel very sexy after having a baby. For us ladies, this is a pretty insecure time. Our bodies during pregnancy are no longer our own. Parts stretch and move in ways that shock and alarm us. Sometimes it's difficult to enjoy sex while you're pregnant. It certainly requires more creativity, especially in late pregnancy. After the baby is born, we instantly want our bodies back. Seeing our toes again is not enough. We desperately want to get back in our jeans. My experience is, after the mandatory six-week post-delivery no-sex zone, husbands desperately want to get back into their wives' jeans too.

When you're nursing, stretch-marked, and not sleeping at night, you mostly want to hide under the covers instead of hitting the sheets. Your body does not feel like your own. When you're already sharing it with the baby, it's tough to also share it with your husband. But you need to. Men, you can do a lot to help us ladies in this area. Reminding us we're beautiful and telling us how you appreciate the sacrifice we've made to carry a child is life giving. Your assurance during this time of self-doubt shows love and is an investment in your marriage. It's necessary to support your wife as she transitions from baby receptacle to wife and mother.

There are a number of steps we ladies can take to make this transition. Nursing is a wonderful way to burn calories and get back into shape. It's not for everyone, but it's valuable for both you and the baby. Exercise is another way to start feeling better and lose some baby weight. This can be done alone or along with your spouse—or even with the baby. Some of my favorite activities when Mikayla was small were to walk with her in the backpack, rollerblade with her in the stroller, and bike ride with her in the baby seat.

One of the advantages to our new home was more space to exercise. When the winter came, I now had a place to workout without fighting the snow. I especially enjoyed the days when Erv would join me for my Denise Austin videos. He's always been my favorite exercise partner (although I'm pretty sure he prefers our current P90X and Insanity workouts to the Denise Austin days). Even in our bigger place, the two of us would frequently crash into each other as we sweated our way around the room. Those shared experiences not only helped our health but also improved our physical intimacy and sense of connection as a couple.

Sex is a great way to burn calories too. While we wish it burned more, I guess that's another good reason to make it a frequent event. If you wait until your body is perfect to enjoy each other physically, you'll be waiting a long time. Don't believe a lie stating you are unattractive. You do not need a perfectly flat belly or stretch-mark free skin for your spouse to find you sexy. He or she loves you as a person. You are now the parent of his or her child. That in itself is incredibly attractive!

When you own a multi-family home, having renters does add a new dynamic to your marriage. You will make some sacrifices in the area of personal privacy. For us, this was well worth the residual income. We inherited a renter in one first floor apartment from the previous owners, and Erv's cousin moved into the other apartment. The rental earnings were enough to cover our mortgage, and we enjoyed living in our larger, new home for free.

Even with the semi-lack of privacy, the rental income was a welcome gift to our marriage. Erv started looking for ways to increase our return on investment even more. After comparing interest rates, he decided to take the subsidized loans he was offered for his Ph.D. program. While we were opposed to incurring debt, we would take this money and pay extra on our mortgage each month. Since extra payments are applied directly toward the principle, the interest paid would be cut, as well as the length of the mortgage. The interest rate on our mortgage was higher than the interest rate on the school loans. It made sense to use one to pay off the other. We knew this wasn't our long-term home. When we sold it in the future, we could use the income from the sale to pay off the school loans, and we'd have saved thousands of dollars along the way. This increased savings rate was energizing to our marriage.

We've found most people don't consider living in a multi-family home a viable housing option. For us, it has been one of our best money savers. It has also been a wonderful way to share our lives with others. We enjoyed having Erv's cousin downstairs and our other renter, Suzy, was a delight to know. She became a wonderful friend and an adopted aunt to Mikayla. We would occasionally have our renters over for dinner or invite them for special events like Christmas parties and BBQs. An added bonus to developing a relationship with our tenants was rent paid on time and infrequent complaints about minor issues like clogged toilets and burned out light bulbs.

When you read a real estate listing, "good condition" really means "not good." Our house was affordable because it was in "good condition." Our home was considered a handyman's special. There were several significant issues needing to be addressed. Our goal was to fix up the house while living in it so we could resell it for a profit. We've found that doing work ourselves is a considerable money saver.

We painted both the interior and the exterior of the house. Paint is my favorite renovation tool. You make the biggest impact for the smallest investment. This is especially true if you aren't fussy about color. If you're flexible, you can get mis-tinted paint for a fraction of the cost of a custom color. This is paint that was tinted for a previous customer, but the customer decided not to buy it once it was mixed. This paint is not usually on display, so you'll need to ask a store what they have.

When painting the exterior, we bought in bulk. Buying paint in a five gallon bucket is cheaper than buying it in one gallon cans. With large projects, this is the way to go. We also increased the value of our discount home with lots of help from our general contractor and father-in- law. He installed a clearance piece of linoleum in the kitchen and replaced the 30-year-old roof. He was extremely generous to us loaning his tools, his time, and his trade.

You may not have a contractor for a father-in-law, but you'd be surprised at what you can accomplish on your own. Before hiring someone to do work around your house, do a little research. There are countless how-to videos online, teaching everything from laying ceramic tile to installing crown molding. There are so many ways to increase the value of your home by investing your own sweat equity. Places like Home Depot even offer free classes on home improvement skills. You'll save thousands on most jobs by doing it yourself. Working on these projects together was yet another great adventure for Erv and me. Working side by side created a great bond between us during a busy, stressful stage of our marriage. Accomplishing a task together gave us something to celebrate!

ERV'S TAKE

DIY in the age of YouTube videos is even easier than it was for us. Sometimes you have more time than money, so learn something new and build lasting memories. It won't always turn out perfect, but what does the first time around? There is a satisfaction that comes from accomplishing a goal or completing a project. You feel good about yourself and co-laborers. You create stories and points of connection that last through the years. You know you've succeeded when a week, month, year, or decade later one of you starts a conversation with, "Remember when…"

The spring semester was wrapping up, and my pregnant status was coming to an end. Two weeks before my due date, the contractions commenced. Surprised, I called my mom, who arrived two hours later. We took 20-month-old Mikayla for long walks in the stroller, played marathon games of Monopoly, and watched late night movies. When things did not progress, I made myself try and get some sleep. By 5 a.m., I was too uncomfortable to rest. I got up and took a walk while everyone else slept. I had left a note and my mom came and found me an hour later. She couldn't sleep either. I waited as long as possible before going to the hospital. Mom stayed home with Mikayla when Erv and I finally headed out. Our daughter Brianna took as long to arrive as her big sister had. It was 8:38 p.m. before she made her debut. Mom delayed putting Mikayla to bed so she could meet her new sister. They arrived at the hospital just as Brianna was born.

Mikayla was Brianna's very first visitor. She climbed up onto the bed with me, admiring her little sister. She was fascinated with Brianna's eyes. In fact, we had to keep her from poking them out of Brianna's little head. Just a toddler herself, Mikayla longed to touch all things bright and shiny. This special sister visit was brief as I hadn't even delivered the placenta yet. A nurse escorted Mikayla and my mother out to the crowded waiting room with the rest of our friends and family. I'm so glad we had Mikayla and my mom come in for that brief visit immediately after Brianna was born. Once they left the room, things went terribly wrong.

CHAPTER SEVENTEEN

LOVE AND OTHER NEAR-DEATH EXPERIENCES

When we lost our first baby, we learned that emergencies test our relationship. When we experience something tragic or difficult together, it bonds us in a unique way. The intensity of the moment sears the emotions of the trial into our soul. When we share these feelings with another person, we become attached to them in a powerful way.

Survivors of a car crash, fellow soldiers, and emergency workers experience this. Couples experience this as well when they face something extremely difficult. For some married couples, the tragedy forges an even stronger bond between them. For other couples, the intensity tears them apart. This remains one of my greatest fears.

Our daughter Mikayla, who is now a teenager, was recently in a car accident. We arrived at the emergency room to find her strapped to a backboard, laying on a gurney in the hallway. There was no blood. No broken bones. Not one single bruise on her body. In fact, she lay there smiling, grateful to see us. But it was still scary. Just the thought of losing her shook us both. For a moment I allowed myself to think about her being gone. I know the intensity of losing a child is enough to turn spouses against one another. I found myself praying Erv and I would never have to experience that tragedy. The scare we had at Brianna's birth was enough.

I remember being confused when Mikayla was first born. After holding her for about five minutes, they took her away from me so I could deliver the placenta. I consider myself to be a pretty good listener, but I didn't remember hearing about this in childbirth classes. In all of the movies we watched, the woman went through labor, the baby was born, and that was the end. I did not recall anyone delivering a placenta. I was so exhausted after 20 hours of labor, I was not interested in delivering anything else. Ignoring my lack of enthusiasm, the nurses told me to push. After three good pushes, the placenta was out, and they had put Mikayla back in my arms. It turned out to be no big deal. This was not what happened with Bri.

During Mikayla's visit with baby Brianna, my doctor patiently waited. She knew this was an important moment for our family, but she was concerned I hadn't yet delivered the placenta. As soon as Mikayla and my mom left the room, I began pushing. Nothing happened. I pushed some more. Still nothing. Another 30 minutes passed, and the placenta was not budging. I was frustrated and tired but oblivious to the danger I was in. Erv, however, had noticed the atmosphere in the room changing. Our doctor's face had gone from calm and joyful to stressed and concerned. Erv also watched as a large basin placed underneath me was filling up with blood. He wasn't training to become a medical doctor, but he knew this was not good. He kept his worried thoughts to himself and spoke only calm, encouraging words to me.

About an hour after Brianna's birth, everything in the room changed. Suddenly, there was a flurry of activity as medical personnel rushed into the room, surrounding me. I was being given medication as my doctor explained the placenta would need to be surgically removed. I had lost too much blood, and they couldn't wait any longer. Depending on the damage to my uterus, she may have to perform a hysterectomy. My brain struggled to process what was happening. I had just celebrated the birth of a healthy baby girl. Now I was being rushed to the operating room and may never give birth again. As they wheeled me away in my hospital bed, I searched for Erv. I could not see him anywhere. I lost consciousness and everything went black.

I woke up confused and disoriented. A nurse offered me a sip of orange juice from a straw. Where was I? Where were Erv and my baby? I spotted a clock on the wall. It was one in the morning. I had missed hours of precious bonding time with Brianna. I was sad and angry. The orange juice nurse disappeared, and I needed her. I wanted to see my husband…and my baby… and my mom… and my husband's mom…and his dad. I wanted to know if I still had a uterus. Would I ever give birth again? Why did this happen to me? Where was the blasted orange juice nurse? Was there a button somewhere I could push? Maybe I should just yell. I was too tired to yell. I just closed my eyes and prayed.

I felt someone touch my left arm, and I looked up. It wasn't the orange juice nurse. It was Erv. Hooray!! I felt an incredible sense of relief. He had been in the nursery, feeding Brianna. He had been holding her and caring for her the past few hours. Our family and friends had met Brianna in the nursery, and now they had all gone home. Our baby was healthy and doing well. And I still had a uterus. They were able to remove the placenta without even doing surgery. I was relieved and thankful. And I wanted to see my baby.

Erv stayed with me in the recovery room for about 30 minutes. He shared his own experience over the past few hours. It was frightening for him to see me fading away right in front of him. He was thankful for our new baby, but he did not want to lose his wife. He found himself struggling with fear and anger. He didn't want to sacrifice me for Brianna. Then as he sat holding her in the nursery, being the very first to ever feed her, they bonded in special way. He was so grateful to know he could keep us both.

When you almost lose someone you love, you value him or her in a surprising new way. I once dreamed Erv died of a heart attack while out running. A friend had recently gone through this exact experience and I lived it out myself in my dream. I woke up panicked and sweaty. Instantly, I could feel Erv's body curled up against mine. I turned toward him and wrapped my arm around him, my head against his chest. I just listened to his heart beating, reminding me he was still alive. All day and all week, I valued him in a new way. The very thought of losing him grew my appreciation for him.

I don't believe it's healthy to live our lives in constant fear, but I do believe it's beneficial to value the frailty of life. We have no guarantee of spending the next ten, twenty, or forty years with our spouse. We promise them a lifetime when we speak our vows but all we can truly give them is today. There is a chance we will still be by their side tomorrow, but it is only a possibility. When we view the future with such awe and appreciation, we value our spouse in a new way each morning.

This may sound ridiculous, but I always save my most recent voice mail from Erv. I don't assume I'll hear his voice again. If I lose him, this will be a precious treasure. I'm not a paranoid person. I simply cherish the present. It makes me value my husband more. It's hard to stay angry when you remember this could be the last conversation you ever have.

In a hospital nursery, Erv was reminded of the frailty of my life. At a time when the stress and pressure in our marriage was increasing, he was filled with greater joy. Bri and I were both here to stay, at least for another day. The challenge of providing for a growing family was eclipsed by gratitude.

They moved me to a private room and sent Erv home to get some rest. I drifted in and out of sleep, longing to see our new baby. I could barely remember what she looked like. My time with her had been so short. Would I recognize her when I finally got to hold her? Would she be willing to nurse after having a bottle? I wished I were able to get up and go see her.

At 4 a.m., they finally brought little Brianna to my room. It was dark, and I could barely make out her face at first. She was so tiny and perfectly adorable. She nursed without issue and slept peacefully in my arms. In the morning, they brought me to a shared room in the maternity ward, and Brianna was brought in shortly after. I spent the day in a fog, introducing baby Brianna to more friends and family. I still felt extremely weak. The doctors kept a close eye on my blood count, and by the afternoon, they recommended I have a transfusion. I wasn't improving. All day my visitors had commented on how pale I was. My mom said I looked "white as a sheet." Erv and I were both nervous about me getting a transfusion. Did the benefits outweigh the risks? Was this really necessary? Erv's blood is type O, making him a universal donor. We investigated the option of Erv giving me his own blood. We were told this was not an option. As the hours passed, my condition only grew worse. We finally decided to accept the blood transfusion. Erv said goodbye to me for the night as they began giving me a stranger's blood. Almost immediately, I was feeling better. My energy returned, and I was anxious to go home the next morning.

At 8 a.m., Erv picked me up from the hospital with a brand new air conditioner sticking out awkwardly from the trunk of our car. "I guess I'm not going to surprise you when we get home," Erv joked. "Here's your baby gift." On this hot, sticky day at the end of June, an air conditioner was a beautiful sight to behold! It was an extravagant gift that I knew was costly for Erv to give. When we arrived at home, there was also a beautiful bouquet of roses picked from our garden on the dining room table. It was surrounded by scribbled "pictures" drawn by big sister Mikayla. I sat on the couch with my baby girls while Erv installed the shiny, new air conditioner. I had so much to be thankful for!

ERV'S TAKE

Some moments demand extravagance. It is okay to splurge at times. If you've followed our advice, you will have the money when those moments arise. Try to be lavish and generous with your treasures, talents, and time. It can become natural to hoard and skimp – worrying there will never be enough time, opportunity, or money. The lesson of giving is one of a life free from the worry of limited supply and embraces the concept of abundance. Abundance allows us to give freely and cheerfully, not expecting anything in return or fearing there will never be enough.

CHAPTER EIGHTEEN

CAMPING CATASTROPHES

When we dream of having grand adventures, we know it will cost us. The more awesome the adventure, the more we will have to pay for it. As young parents of two small children, we didn't have much money to spend on exotic vacations or extended escapes. Yet, some of the greatest experiences we've ever had have been innovative and inexpensive.

Don't limit your enjoyment as a couple by assuming you have to spend a lot of money on your adventures. Consider alternatives allowing you to get away without coming home to unwanted credit card bills. Do you have to stay in a four star hotel? Do you have to travel out of state or out of the country to escape the day-to-day grind? Not necessarily.

ERV'S TAKE

It was always exciting to come home from my seminary studies. Carrie would have some surprise waiting for me. Once I went on a scavenger hunt all over our apartment. As I searched out each clue I grew closer to the final prize: my wonderful wife, waiting for me, with the warmest of embraces.

In twenty years, she hasn't stopped surprising me. Just this year she arranged a high adventure kidnapping for my birthday, complete with CIA agents, men in black, a mob boss' threat, and dinner on the roof of our garage.

For us, some of our favorite adventures have been just outside our door. More specifically, they've been inside a tent. I know, camping is not for everyone, but hear me out. Stretching outside your comfort zone and trying something new (like camping) can bring great energy to your relationship. Having to work together on setting up the tent and cooking outdoors is a unique bonding experience. Overcoming adversity as a couple encourages problem solving together and a sense of team. It's one of the best bonding factors of camping.

When Brianna was just 4 weeks old, we ventured out on our first camping trip after the girls were born. We were excited to introduce our baby girls to one of our favorite activities. Our destination was Old Orchard Beach in Maine, the same place we were engaged five years earlier. We would meet up with some dear friends from Oneonta, Julianne and Russ. They were fellow campers and parents of six-month-old Ethan.

I was nervous about camping with babies, but I had done my research. I read newborns were great camping companions. They slept most of the time, and when awake, they were not mobile, so they were easy to manage. Since Brianna was nursing, we would not need to pack bottles or special food for her. Her Pack-n-Play (inherited from Mikayla) fit in our new tent (bought on clearance as an anniversary gift to each other). The way we had raised Mikayla thus far, she was used to sleeping anywhere. We brought my old sleeping bag from my girl scouting days (literally 20 years earlier) and figured she would be just fine.

Erv and I prefer to travel light. As I packed up our car for the four-day outing, I was conscious to bring as little as possible. Mikayla was just beginning to talk and didn't give me much feedback on packing. To save space, I left her big, bulky teddy bear (cleverly named "Bear") home in favor of a smaller, stuffed blue horse she had enjoyed as an infant. Once we got to the campsite, 300 miles from home, she asked for Bear. Then she cried for Bear. Then she screamed for Bear. We had been at the campsite for five minutes. We were in trouble.

"You didn't pack Bear? Her bear she sleeps with every night! What were you thinking?" Erv asked, frustrated.

"I was thinking we've got four people, two car sets, three sleeping bags, a tent, a cooler, and a Pack-n-Play in our car, and I wanted to save space. I'm sorry." I felt foolish for making this tactical error.

It's amazing how quickly we can turn on one another in a crisis. One moment we're allies and the next, we're enemies. It's easy to allow the stress of a situation become more important than your relationship. We question our partner's actions or motives. We become defensive instead of open-minded. We see limited options instead of new possibilities.

If you can remain calm under pressure, it will serve your marriage well. When your partner is upset, try to be the supportive one. Don't allow your emotions to take over. It's best if at least one of you keeps a level head. In this situation, neither of us was calm. We were quick to judge. Quick to criticize. It took a while for us to transition from being problem oriented to solutions oriented.

Not able to run home and grab Mikayla's precious teddy bear, we went into problem solving mode. We headed to the on-site camp store to see if they sold any stuffed animals. They didn't. It's no fun to cuddle with a bag of charcoal or firewood, the staple items in the store. I tried to comfort her with the little stuffed blue horse I'd packed. It didn't work. That's when we discovered the playground. We brought Mikayla to the swings, and she was quickly distracted from thinking about her teddy bear. Crisis averted—at least until bedtime.

Our friends met up with us in the late afternoon, and we enjoyed dinner cooked over our camp stove. Mikayla was covered with dirt from head to toe after playing on the ground while the adults visited. Baby Bria and our friends' baby Ethan sat side-by-side in their car seats under my long bridal veil, doubling as a mosquito net. I cleaned up Mikayla the best I could with baby wipes, and we put all three kids to bed. The babies fell asleep quickly in their Pack-n-Plays.

Mikayla was a different story. As the adults sat around the campfire sipping hot cocoa, Mikayla started whining, "I want Bear. Can't sleep without Bear!" Not wanting the babies to wake up, Erv went quickly into our tent to settle Mikayla. He never came back out. When I snuck into our dark tent to check on them a few minutes later, my Girl Scout sleeping bag was empty, and Mikayla was sound asleep on Erv's chest.

Erv was half-asleep and encouraged me to go back out and

enjoy our friends. After an hour of chatting around the fire, I rejoined my little family in our tent for the night. I had just fallen asleep when Brianna started to cry. Not wanting to wake up the whole campground, I quickly lifted her out of the Pack-n-Play and started to nurse her. Or at least I tried to. She was not interested. Instead of nursing peacefully in the dark, she fussed and cried.

Mikayla and Erv woke up to the crying, and I quickly left the tent. Her cries seemed only magnified by the dark openness of the forest surrounding us. I tried walking with her, bouncing her, rocking her in my arms. She continued to cry. Her cries echoed off the rocks and trees. It was the loudest crying I had ever heard. We were surrounded by tents full of sleeping families. I needed to do something and fast. I suddenly spotted temporary salvation. Our 1988 Reliant K car. At least in there, the crying would be muffled. I slipped into the backseat with screaming Brianna and shut the door.'

Once seated inside, I tried again to nurse Bri. She fussed and cried but eventually settled down. I'm sure it helped that I was finally relaxed, not worried about waking the world in the middle of the night. As Brianna nursed, I dozed off sitting upright in the car. I was so tired after a long day of driving and a stressful afternoon fretting over Mikayla's missing teddy bear. I longed to sleep stretched out in my sleeping bag. Brianna started to fuss once more and then full-out cry. Not again, I thought. At least this time, we were confined to the car.

We stayed there all night. Brianna would cry, nurse, settle down and then cry again. This pattern continued all night long. I was thankful to pass her off to Erv in the morning. Our second night was a repeat performance. Brianna and I both spent the night in the car. By the second morning, we cut our trip short and headed for home.

I don't recommend camping with babies.

CHAPTER NINETEEN

LIVE FOR TODAY, PLAN FOR TOMORROW

When we have a negative experience as a couple, we are quick to abandon anything remotely resembling the experience. We don't ever want to go through the same heartache and struggle again. After our first-ever camping-with-children outing turned into a colossal failure, we were wary of a repeat performance.

It's hard to discern as a couple if the experience we had is one to be completely avoided or if it's something valuable we can learn from and try again. Hardship is impossible to avoid. So many circumstances are outside of our control. Particularly with small children, the risks are high and the outcomes are rarely what we expect when making plans.

Don't make a quick decision in the moment when things go wrong. Maybe one day you'll love that particular activity. Many new experiences come with a learning curve requiring an open mind and a willing heart. Particularly when the outing is something near and dear to your spouse's heart, it's important you remain open to trying again. You show incredible kindness toward your spouse when you're willing to try something they love once again.

We were curious to know if this camping disaster was merely a fluke or actually characteristic of camping with kids. Instead of giving up on the idea completely, we decided to give it another try the following summer.

I had completed a busy year of campus ministry with two babies. Our hand-me-down double stroller made the rounds across campus. Erv was quite busy between working, taking classes, being a teaching assistant, and studying for qualifying exams. Once the stress of those challenging tests passed, he began research for his dissertation. He suddenly realized why most people quit their Ph.D. programs during this phase. During that year he also switched jobs again, from working at the county to assisting a financial planner. The new position gave him more flexibility, allowing him to teach part-time and giving him more experience in his field. By the end of the jam-packed school year, we were anxious to get away to our favorite escape—the outdoors.

After experiencing our Maine camping fiasco along with us, our friends Russ and Julianne suggested a different destination. We joined them at a family camp in the Adirondack Mountains of New York. We wouldn't be as far from home, and this facility had a host of programs to accommodate families. There were sing-a-longs and rodeos and rafting trips. It sounded like an ideal place to pursue adventure as a family. The price was a bit higher than we would typically pay for camping, but it was still much cheaper than a hotel vacation. Brianna had been sleeping through the night for months, and Mikayla's bear was safely packed in the car. We left in our crowded little car with high hopes—confident this would be a successful family camping trip.

This is one of many occasions where Erv and I learned the importance of reading the fine print. I hate reading fine print. So does Erv. Neither of us are particularly detail oriented. We both tend to jump into situations and figure out the details later. Yet we've learned at least one of us needs to actually read the directions before assembling large items. This is usually me. Someone also needs to read the fine print on contracts. That's usually Erv. As we reviewed the paperwork provided by the family camp, Erv noticed some unpleasant fine print.

There were many unique adventure opportunities offered at the camp. Unfortunately, they all required an additional fee. Erv and I were forced to decide which one activity we would pay for out of the five we had selected when we chose to come to this camp. While the children were quite content with playground swings and ice cream cones, Erv and I were disappointed. We were excited to go white water rafting, horseback riding, and rappelling. These activities were the reason we'd chosen this campground.

It was tempting to go with the original plan and do everything we wanted. Technically, we had the money to do all the activities we wished. But we had a goal. Now that we owned our own home, we were saving to purchase our own business. If we didn't say no to tempting opportunities now, we would not be able to say yes to better opportunities later.

As a couple, this is a difficult decision to make. Most families will choose the immediate gratification of doing everything they want right now. You work hard for your money and want to enjoy yourselves today. This is a perfectly normal expectation.

However, you must consider what you want in the future. Do you always want to live paycheck to paycheck? Do you want your marriage to be characterized by being strapped for cash? If so, do everything you want right now, in this moment.

ERV'S TAKE

You can either make decisions that reflect your priorities, or impulsive decisions that will set your priorities. You can't say something is important and act as if it isn't with conviction and honesty. Sometimes life's toughest decision is between two good things. The question becomes, "Which is best?" This is when you truly see for yourself what you prioritize and value. We absolutely love adventure, but not at any cost and not above all else. We also value each other and joint decisions help us affirm this truth. What do you and your spouse value? How are your actions and decisions reflecting your priorities?

What sacrifices are you willing to make today so you can experience even greater adventures tomorrow? We had big dreams and goals ahead of us. No one was going to hand us the money to make them happen. If we wanted to see ourselves as business owners in the future, we needed to live more carefully in the present. We made the choice to live without our immediate wants in favor of our future desires. This had been our philosophy for years, and it has served our family well.

It's amazing how the stress from home follows you and only

becomes magnified when you travel. While we made financial progress throughout the year, our relationship had suffered. It felt like Erv was always gone or busy studying. I was juggling working and taking care of two little ones, while also cooking and cleaning our home. We both felt there was more to do than we had enough time for. There were days I would get resentful and make a list of all of the things I had done throughout the day, seeking to prove to Erv that I was harder working than he was. He would then make his own list of everything he had done all day, and it was just as long as mine. We both fought off resentment and struggled to put ourselves in each other's shoes. This family camping trip was meant to be a break from the busy schedules and long days apart. That's not exactly what happened.

Making yet another financial sacrifice while on vacation caused a darkness to settle over our campsite. Erv was moody and distant. I was anxious, not wanting to increase the disappointment. Erv retreated to the tent to take a nap. I struggled to keep the girls occupied while trying to cook our dinner. Mikayla was not yet three years old and mildly helpful. She could fetch plates from the car or ketchup from the cooler, but she was more interested in stacking rocks into interesting formations on the ground than she was in helping me prepare supper.

Bria had just turned one and was learning to walk. She tottered around the campsite, using the tent poles and picnic benches to steady herself. She was basically a walking train wreck. Her preferred direction of movement, however, was up. In just ten minutes, she had managed to climb up onto the picnic table, scatter the paper plates, and dump out all of the Kool-Aid. As she scooted across the table toward the camp stove, I yelled to Erv for help. I needed a second set of hands, quickly.

Still groggy from his nap, Erv stumbled out of the tent. He picked Brianna up from the table and placed her on the ground by Mikayla and her pile of rocks. "Play with your sister," he said, and he grabbed a book and settled into a lawn chair by the campfire. Mikayla swiftly placed herself between Brianna and the precious pile of rocks, not wanting her baby sister to ruin her elaborate creation.

"No Bri Bri! No!" Mikayla scolded. Brianna was trying to reach the precious rocks. I could tell Mikayla was ready to swat at her.

"Mikayla. Keep your hands to yourself!" I corrected. Though it would have been best to physically put some space between the girls and give Brianna something different to play with, I already had a big mess to clean up, and I didn't want to leave the camp stove unattended. "Share with your sister!" I called to her. I was doubtful this would work, but I hoped so. What I was really hoping was Erv would get involved in this situation, but I never asked. Wasn't it obvious? He continued reading his book.

I started cleaning up the Kool-Aid and the spaghetti pot boiled over, putting out the fire on the camp stove. Brianna reached for another rock, and Mikayla screamed. As I struggled to get the stove relit, I said to Erv, "Aren't you going to help me?" My resentment from the many days spent juggling babies while preparing dinner as Erv studied in the living room back home came flooding over me. "You are so lazy!" I complained. Erv stood up and walked toward me. He kept right on walking, right out of the campsite. Words spoken in anger are rarely effective.

I managed to relight the camp stove, feed the girls dinner, and put them to bed. When Erv came back, he was hurt. "How could you call me lazy," he asked me, baffled and insulted. "I work two jobs while going to school full time. I never go out to dinner or out for drinks with the other students after class. I always come right home so I can help you. You're always on edge, worried I'm going to be upset at anything you say. You're not even fun anymore!"

Now I was hurt. Not fun? Me, not fun?! Who could he possibly be talking about? If I were to make a list of my defining characteristics, I would put "fun" near the top. I love to have fun, and I enjoy making ordinary activities fun for other people. This was the ultimate insult. But as we sat in silence staring at the campfire, I knew he was right. I had become paranoid about making him angry. The stress of school and work and small children running around was a lot for Erv. I was always trying to insulate him from it. I had stopped speaking my mind, making silly suggestions, and going out of my way to infuse our lives with humor and creativity. I wasn't as fun, and I was the one getting angry. I wouldn't ask for help, but I would be angry when I didn't get it. What started as a bitter argument slowly evolved into a frank and helpful discussion.

The truth is hard to speak, but it's necessary if your marriage is going to last. As spouses, we typically operate at one of two extremes. We are either frequently critical, speaking our mind at all times resulting in hurt because we are too harsh, or we are typically quiet, keeping our opinions to ourselves in hopes of keeping the peace. Neither of these extremes is healthy for your relationship.

On a regular basis, we must speak openly with our spouses. In our marriage, we have a check-up exercise called, "One to Ten." We ask each other how our relationship is going on a scale of one to ten. We both pick a number in our heads before saying it out loud. We share our numbers and then explain why we rated our relationship as we did.

This can be really tough. It's possible one of you believes everything is fine in your relationship when the other person is really dissatisfied. If your personality is at all like mine, it's uncomfortable to complain about what's wrong. You don't want to make it worse by bringing attention to it. Yet, if you don't address it, it will become worse. As a spouse, it's difficult to repair a problem you don't know about. By committing to openly evaluate your relationship on a regular basis, you ensure problems are addressed before they lead to irreconcilable differences.

This "One to Ten" exercise also provides an objective way to share concerns with your spouse. This is not a gripe session where you verbally abuse your spouse, telling them everything you believe to be wrong about them. Words are not expressed in anger or with malice. This is a planned discussion where you quantify your feelings with a number. The number represents the health of the relationship rather than being an evaluation of one individual spouse. When you state the number, you own your part of whatever challenges your marriage is facing.

Many times when you share your number, this exercise will simply serve as an affirmation of the health of your marriage. This is encouraging and life giving to your relationship. You may be pleasantly surprised when your spouse feels your marriage is at a 9 or 10. When you're investing so much of yourself into a relationship, it's affirming to hear your spouse say things are going well. Knowing this exercise is coming also helps provide accountability to continually work on your relationship.

While the discussion in our campsite that night was not a formal "One to Ten" discussion, the openness of the argument brought valuable information to light. We didn't resolve every-thing in one single discussion, but we had been honest with one another and were making progress. Erv committed to help out more. I committed to ask for help more and worry less. And I would be intentional about being more fun!

By morning, we were looking forward to our one big excursion on this camping trip. It was timed perfectly after our difficult evening. We had signed up for a trail ride and rodeo. The girls rode in a hay wagon with our friend Julianne and little Ethan while Russ, Erv, and I rode on horseback. It was a beautiful, relaxing tour through the Adirondack wilderness. After our ride, we enjoyed the playground while waiting for the rodeo to begin. Our girls were thrilled when the horses came galloping through the starting gate. We spent the next hour admiring and enjoying the colorful display of courage and talent. By the end of our camping week, Erv was very helpful with the girls, and I was extremely and undeniably fun!

CHAPTER TWENTY

PERSEVERANCE AND PERSPIRATION

Big decisions stress me out. I am more likely to stick with the status quo than to initiate change. This is embarrassing to admit, but it's nonetheless true. It usually takes some outside force to spring me into action when change is needed. This force is often my risk taking, status quo-adverse husband. Once the change is in motion, I embrace the opportunity and am energized by it. Looking back, I always wonder why I didn't leap sooner. This is one of the many reasons I am so glad I married Erv.

Of the various lessons learned on our Adirondack camping trip, one of the less exciting discoveries was that we needed a new car. Our wedding gift, the used K car, was more than a decade old. We had been paying for minor repairs for years, and more small problems kept arising. The right-hand passenger's side door had a broken latch, which we eventually had to tie shut to keep from swinging open when making a right hand turn. Whenever I was the passenger, I had to enter on the drivers' side and then scoot across the bench seat. This was after loading two girls into their car seats, one on either side of the car. I was always exhausted by the time I actually sat down.

But my change-adverse personality was fine with it. I'd become adjusted to the idiosyncrasies of this car. They were known and familiar factors. I preferred to stick with our old, broken car than to go through the hassle and headache of finding a new one. Every car has problems. At least with this car, we knew what they were.

However, with our busy schedules and Erv's new job across town, he really wanted a second car. Our friends Evelyn and Mark had recently bought a new car, and they generously gave their old car to us. It was a sports car with high mileage and only two doors. We enjoyed the luxury of having a second car, although we didn't enjoy paying double for gas and insurance. Erv loved that it was sporty, but it was extremely difficult to get the car seats into it. With the K car in the shop more frequently, the four of us would have to pile into the little sports car. And then the sports car started making funny noises and had an interesting smell. We were waiting to get the K car back from the shop so we could put the sports car in when we got the doomsday call. The engine block was cracked. Unless we wanted to put a new engine in our very old car, we were out of options. We started looking for a new, used car.

I was more than happy to buy a used car instead of a new one. We never had a new car growing up, and I did not feel like we needed one. But I didn't want just any car. We had two small children, and I was hoping to one-day have more. (I did still have a uterus after all!) I was also regularly stuffing college students into our little car. I wanted a mini-van. This was my dream vehicle. Not only did it have more seating, it had more storage for the stroller, Pack-n-Play, portable high chair, and other ba-by-related paraphernalia. It also had more room for camping gear—an issue on our last two outings.

Erv was morally opposed to my plan. He hated mini-vans. He is a man. He believed there was nothing masculine about a mini-van. To him, it felt like selling out. He was already a married father of two in his mid-twenties. Most of his friends were still single and driving new Saturns. He was not going to live like a middle-aged suburbanite, driving around town in a boxy mini-van. That would not happen. I actually believed him.

We came to a compromise. We began looking for a Ford Escort station wagon. This would give us more storage space, but it wasn't a mini-van. Erv could live with this option. I still wanted the extra seating, but I was supportive of this decision. I began searching ads in the local auto sales magazines and called every car dealership in the Albany area. I spent hours making phone calls, doing the research. I created a whole comparison chart outlining the year, mileage, and special features of each available car. We picked the five that fit our budget and seemed like the best deals. We drove to each individual seller or car dealership and test drove them all. We haggled with each seller to get a quote of their best price. Then, we'd make the rounds again, trying to get them to out-bid their competitors. This became a fun game we both enjoyed playing. We had our choices down to two cars when we stopped at a random dealership alongside the road.

I couldn't believe Erv was stopping. It was a small dealership with only five or six cars for sale. All mini-vans! Not an Escort station wagon in sight. As Erv walked me up to the dark grey Dodge Caravan, my eyes lit up like Christmas trees. Not only was this van a good deal with relatively low mileage (meaning less than 100,000 by our definition), it had something I had never seen before. Something I instantly knew would make our lives so much easier. Something I never knew I wanted until I saw them with my very own eyes: built-in car seats! They were located in the second row. They hid away inside the regular seat and then easily flipped down to become safety child seats. There were many times when I would have to take our car seats out of the K car to have room for our college students on the way to an event or to church. With these seats, I wouldn't have to move anything when I had a Campus Ambassadors event. These built-in seats were glorious!

Unfortunately, they were too expensive. Even when we talked the dealer down, this van was $1,000 outside of our price range. We could not buy it. We would not finance it. We would live without it. But we could not bring ourselves to buy anything else. The Ford Escort station wagon we had chosen just could not live up to those built-in car seats. And now with Erv open to a mini-van, I was not satisfied with a station wagon. We prayed and asked God for the mini-van. We knew we couldn't afford it, but we refused to give up hope. We went back to the dealer. He really liked us and wanted to help, but this was his rock bottom price.

It was tempting to finance this car. We could make payments each month and it would fit into our budget. However, this did not fit into our long-range plans. We had been saving money toward our next car for years. This money had been earning interest in our savings account. If we financed the car, we would be paying interest each month instead of earning interest each month. This would not bring us any closer to the ownership of a business. We were both committed to spending only the amount we had saved. Again we decided to forego what we wanted today in favor of gaining something of greater value to us tomorrow.

ERV'S TAKE

"No." It is one of the earliest words we all learn. I seldom like to hear it said to me, even if speaking it to myself. Learning to say "No," or at least "Not now," is a powerful tool for a long marriage. You will have to let go of some immediate pleasures to have the full marriage adventure. "No" is an acceptable answer to something you think you want. If fact, I often say "No" is the second best answer there is.

The summer was coming to an end, and we went on a weekend camping trip with some friends from church. Amy and Jamie were also young parents, their baby Annie was just months younger than Brianna. We shared with them about our disappointment over the mini-van with the built-in car seats. They listened and were empathetic. They may have thought I was ridiculous to be in mourning over lost built-in car seats, but they were compassionate and humored me nonetheless.

While on our trip, Erv and Jamie went swimming in the nearby river. The current was fast, and they could body surf their way downstream with the rushing water. They made several trips down the river before climbing out to join us for dinner, but as Jamie came out of the water, he realized his watch was missing.

This wasn't just any watch. This was his father's very special college graduation present. His father had called it a "man's

watch," and it was a precious gift to Jamie. Erv and Jamie began diving, searching the river bottom for the watch. The current was moving swiftly and it was impossible to see. All they
could do was feel their way along the rocks at the bottom. Amy
joined in the search, and I stayed with three small girls alongside
the river, praying they could accomplish the impossible. They
searched and searched for almost an hour. I started to think this
was pointless and considered suggesting they give up.

I'm not usually a quitter. I'm pretty stubborn, so I typically
fight my way through whatever obstacles are in my way. But this
one, I didn't understand. I had no idea how valuable this watch
was. I would buy a new watch every few years when the leather
band wore out on mine, and I usually paid $10, maybe $20 for
a new one.

Fortunately, Erv was more aware than I was. Though he did
not know the exact cost, he knew this was a valuable gift to Jamie, and he was determined to keep looking. The three of them
were just about to give up when Amy miraculously came up
with the watch in her hand. It was amazing! I couldn't believe
it. I had seriously given up hope. Jamie's watch could have been
anywhere down there, hidden among the rocks. How did she
possibly find it?

Jamie and Amy were grateful we were so supportive of
searching for this treasure. While Erv wasn't the one who actually found the watch, his persistence and dedication kept
them motivated to look until it was found. As we sat around
the campfire, we learned the watch wasn't only a special gift to
Jamie from his dad. It was also a Rolex, worth more than $1,000.
They were so grateful for our help, they offered us the $1,000 we
needed to buy the mini-van of my dreams.

It was not easy to accept such a generous gift. We had struggled with this before. Family members and friends had been helping us for years. Now as married parents, it seemed time to stand on our own. Yet, this gift was given with such appreciation and love. We knew it would be arrogance and pride preventing us from accepting it. With humility and gratitude, we accepted their generous gift and promptly purchased our new mini-van—complete with built-in car seats.

PART FOUR

THE TRAVELING
JOURNEY

CHAPTER TWENTY-ONE

GETAWAY FOR TWO

After two summers of family vacation, Erv decided it was time for just the two of us to get away. He could not have been more right. We kept to our weekly date nights, but our "lazy, no fun" breakdown in the Adirondacks showed us we needed some quality time alone together. Raising two little ones just 20 months apart was rewarding, but also stressful and demanding. A friend once told me during this stage of parenting, "The days are long, but the years are short." We were finding this to be quite true. We were thankful for these precious girls; however, we needed time to focus on each other.

You may have difficulty considering travel without your children. Some folks feel guilty leaving them behind. It's okay for you to experience something wonderful once in a while without your kids. Traveling sans children is a valuable way to stay connected with each other over the 18 years you are raising your child. It's important to enjoy adventures for just the two of you.

You may struggle trusting others to care for your kids in your absence. This is a natural, yet often unrealistic fear. It's valuable for children to experience your leaving and then coming back home to them. It builds trust between you when they realize you always return. It also helps build a sense of independence and confidence in your children. They are not constantly dependent on you and your spouse alone to care for them. They learn to trust other adults whom you have chosen to care for them. This is healthy for them as you cannot be their ever-present source of security. This also builds their faith in God, the true constant source of security in their lives.

Your tandem travel also sends them a powerful message about the strong bond between the two of you. It's important for them to see how much you enjoy being together. This connection you have as a couple reminds them of the stability of your family. Your marriage is the foundation upon which your children build their identity—you will be modeling the joy and adventure of marriage to your kids.

Traveling without your children also does wonders for both your communication and your physical intimacy. Having extended time away allows you to converse without constant interruptions from little ones. Traveling provides opportunities to remember why you fell in love with each other in the first place. The thrill and excitement of travel mirrors the rush of first love back in your dating days. Exploring different locations and experiencing new wonders through travel gives you fresh topics of conversation, infusing your relationship with energy and vitality.

The time alone in a new place also does wonders for your sex life. Enjoying a few days without time constraints allows you to relax. This newly refreshed state ignites your marriage with fresh passion. When you don't need to worry about rushing off to work or putting the kids to bed, you have more time and energy to enjoy your spouse. Being in a new location also ignites your imagination and encourages creativity. Don't be afraid to make a fantasy come true. Instead of dreaming about a romantic encounter, make one happen with your spouse!

Erv and I had always longed to travel internationally. When I was young, I remember staying with a neighbor who had just visited Israel. It sounded fascinating. How exciting to walk in the footsteps of Jesus. Erv had always longed to visit China. He was intrigued by Asian culture and wanted to experience it firsthand. Israel and China were still way outside of our price range, but a different and interesting opportunity opened up to us.

The University at Albany was home to many international students. Several of these students became involved in Campus Ambassadors, and I enjoyed the multi-cultural environment they provided for our group. Unable to travel the world, it was wonderful to see God bring the world to us through our international students. They took turns cooking us traditional meals. We learned various cultural forms of worship and (best of all) they invited us to visit them once they returned to their home countries.

One of these students was Victoria, an exchange student from England. After spending a year with us on campus, she returned home and welcomed us to stay with her family in Oxford. We thought England was an ideal place to start our international travel, considering they speak English. My heritage is primarily British, which added interest for me as well. We would be provided with free food and housing so our greatest expense would be plane fare. We had managed to save enough over the past few years to purchase two plane tickets (if we found a good deal). This seemed like the perfect opportunity—but what about our girls?

When I mentioned this trip option on the phone to my friend Pam, she insisted we pursue it. "You have a free place to stay for 10 days in England?! It's your sixth anniversary, you have to go."

"Yes, but we don't have anyone to take care of the girls. We've tried several options and nothing seems to be working out. Maybe we aren't meant to go," I responded.

"Then I'll watch them!" I couldn't believe what I was hearing. I had asked our parents, but I hadn't even considered asking friends. Taking care of a two-year-old and a three-year-old at the same time? It seemed like too much to ask anyone. Plus, Pam and her husband Mike already had three small children of their own. They would be caring for five children, all under the age of five!

"Are you serious?" I asked.

"Yes. Of course!" Besides the obvious insanity of asking my friend to care for five small children, another problem was that Mike and Pam lived in Chicago, which was—a 12 hour drive from Albany. "No problem," my friend explained. "You guys can drive out here, spend a few days with us, and then fly out from Chicago. We'll keep the girls while you're in England, and then you can fly back here. We can visit a few more days, and then you can drive home. When are you coming?" It was too good to be true! Our friends in Chicago were making a huge sacrifice so we could make our dream of taking an international trip a reality. Meanwhile, Victoria's family was willing to let strangers stay in their home and eat their food all because we ministered to their daughter while she was in a foreign country. With all of these factors coming into perfect alignment, we made plans to celebrate our sixth anniversary overseas—something I would have considered impossible on our wedding day.

Anyone considering a trip to Europe expects it to be expensive. Our trip certainly could have been if it weren't for Victoria's family and their generosity. And yet, there were several other factors within our control to keep our expenses low. The first was purchasing our plane tickets. We didn't work with a travel agent but instead put in bids at a variety of Internet travel sites. If your dates are flexible, you can save hundreds of dollars per international ticket. We knew we wanted to be in England for our anniversary, but otherwise, our dates were open.

We flew coach, and we didn't check any bags. It felt wonderful to pack everything we needed into two small suitcases fitting in the overhead bin. After lugging bulky baby supplies everywhere, we felt incredibly free. Packing this light does require a bit of planning (and wearing some of your clothes more than once), but it makes traveling more convenient and affordable.

Once in country, whenever we weren't traveling along with Victoria's family in their car, we used public transportation. We were staying in Oxford but took a bus into London for a day. While there, we purchased another ticket for an all-day, hop on, hop off, double-decker bus tour. This allowed us to travel all over the city, seeing the sights for one inclusive price. We visited beautiful cathedrals, bridges, and museums. We only went inside a building if it was free to enter—and many of them were. We enjoyed wandering through the corridors, admiring the extraordinary architecture.

I was especially excited to visit St. Paul's cathedral. It was six pounds each to enter, so we opted to enjoy our bagged lunch on the majestic steps out front instead. After lunch, we fed the pigeons our leftovers just like the bird lady in Mary Poppins. This felt like experiencing St. Paul's to us! Our one splurge of the day was a visit to the Tower of London. We enjoyed this tour but spent most of the time evaluating if it was worth the 12 pounds each. Not very impressed with the crown jewels or the ancient torture chambers, we decided we had overspent on this tour. Our experience in general with tourist attractions is they over promise and under deliver.

The priceless part of this adventure was experiencing all of the new sights and sounds together for the very first time. Making new discoveries as a couple was exhilarating to us. The absolute highlight of our day in London was strolling along the River Thames, admiring Big Ben and The House of Parliament across the water. We talked effortlessly, enjoying the freedom to roam and wander wherever we pleased. This was exactly what our relationship needed. We felt like we were back in college dating again.

In Oxford the next day, we signed up for a free walking tour. We enjoyed learning the history of the city while meandering through the colleges, streets, and gardens. In the evening, we watched a performance of *Macbeth* in one of the college courtyards. The ticket price included a cup of mulled cider, and the performance under the stars was absolutely magical. If you ever visit Oxford in the summer, we highly recommend a courtyard play.

We spent the next day, our anniversary, in Oxford again. We wandered through the quaint little stores on the main street looking to make a small purchase commemorating our visit. While browsing through a tea shop, I smiled to myself as I heard Pachelbel's *Canon in D* playing. This was our wedding march, and it was playing on our anniversary! When I pointed this out to Erv, he directed me to look out the window. I thought the music was coming through the store's speaker system, but it was actually coming from outside!

We hurried out of the shop to find a string quartet playing our wedding march right in the street. As we moved closer to enjoy the beautiful live music, Erv wrapped his arms around me. In dream-like fashion, the musicians began walking in circles around us as they played the familiar melody. This was the perfect anniversary gift. Instead of an overpriced trinket, God had provided us with a priceless memory. All the trouble we went through to travel, just the two of us, was worth it in that single moment.

ERV'S TAKE

Our trip to England and Scotland was delightful. We all need romance and special shared memories to bind our hearts together. Sometimes the memories are shared struggles and loss, but we also need shared memories of joyful experiences together. For us, the trip was a dream come true, and for a short time we experienced a wonderful world, foreign to our own. We stayed with friends, in modest hostels, and at bed and breakfasts. We visited beautiful attractions, but often opted for the free external view, because we knew at this time in our life this is what we could afford. And to be honest, what we were experiencing was amazing – why ruin it by trying to have what we couldn't afford?

One of my favorite memories was a walk through

the Cotswolds hills. Carrie was like a child at Disney World, having stepped onto the set of a movie or magical fantasyland.

One way to be wise with money is to avoid the trap of always wanting just a little more than is allowed or affordable. It fosters discontentment. It teaches us to under-appreciate what we can have, and struggle with the sense that we always need just a little bit more. It's important to recognize what you do have.

We have found experiences like this to be the best gifts we can give each other. I do have a few possessions holding special meaning, but my memories are far more precious. By investing in unique experiences together, we have built a storehouse of remembrances we could never replace. To associate so many incredible opportunities with Erv makes him all the more precious to me. He is the common link to my most cherished memories.

On our final day in Oxford, Victoria invited us to enjoy one of her favorite English past times—punting. We rented boats for a small fee at one of the University colleges along the River Chawell. We each took turns standing at the stern of the boat, a long, heavy pole in our hands. We used the pole to push off the bottom of the river and propel the boat forward.

This looks easy, and the other boaters going by seemed to be effortlessly moving forward. I could not wait to try it. I immediately sent us crashing into the left riverbank, then the right riverbank, and then back into the left. It seemed impossible to keep the boat moving straight ahead. My turn was cut short. Erv took over and managed to keep us moving straight ahead. This was one of those moments when it's best if you can just laugh at your ridiculously uncoordinated self. I am an expert at this!

One of the best ways to infuse your marriage with adventure is to try things you've never done before. Routine may be comfortable and familiar, but it also breeds boredom in your relationship. When you experience something for the first time, it triggers excitement. Having new experiences, while traveling or right at home, brings vitality to your relationship. Don't be afraid to look foolish or make mistakes by trying something you know nothing about. Laughing at my failed punting attempt was entertaining for both of us.

After five days of enjoying Oxford, Bath, and the Cotswolds hills with Victoria and her family, it was time to venture out on our own. We purchased discount tickets for the train (by European standards we were still student age), and headed north. We love traveling by train. Not only is it economical, it's a wonderful way to see the countryside. The views are magnificent, and you meet some pretty interesting people.

Our first stop was in the fabled town of York. We only had a few hours to visit, so we decided to tour the town from atop the city walls. York has more miles of intact walls than any other city in England, and we wanted to capitalize on this unique experience. We pretended to be armed soldiers protecting our territory as we peered out of the arrow slits in the walls, sneaking across narrow passages and hiding from the enemy. It was great fun. We felt like a couple of rebellious college students on summer vacation.

This is one of our most important travel tips for couples. Do not act your age. Not only does acting young sometimes provide discounted tickets for travel, it increases the fun factor in your relationship. Embrace the freedom of being someplace where absolutely no one knows who you really are. You can let your imagination run wild and act out any crazy scenario you like. Don't feel the need to obey social expectations. Enjoy being playful together. Race one another to the nearest street corner. Slide down the banisters in the railway station. Enjoy an entire meal mimicking your waiter's accent. You might receive some strange looks and, if you're lucky, have your photo taken by a complete stranger. (I love it when that happens, and to be honest, it happens a lot!)

You don't need to break any laws or be rude to your international hosts. You can enjoy the opportunity to be the kids instead of the one always watching the kids. Age is a matter of attitude—the only limits to your level of enjoyment are the ones you put on yourself. Who says you can't dive at the glass floor at the top of the CN Tower? Why do we assume we can't pose with the mannequins in the chic window display? Take a few risks and enjoy the adventure. Don't wait for something exciting to happen to you. Make something awesome happen together.

Our next stop was Berwick-Upon-Tweed, a charming coastal town along the border of England and Scotland. The city is surrounded by beautiful Elizabethan walls. While it was still daylight, we explored the little city and the beautiful coastline. It was cold and windy, but Erv was especially excited to see the ocean. We even spotted a few seals playing in the water. We stopped at a charming pub along a side street for a delicious supper with the locals.

We spent the night in a charming little bed and breakfast, our favorite place to stay outside of a tent. Our housing included a traditional Northumberland breakfast, which was huge. I could barely finish my meal of eggs, ham, biscuits, and other things I could not identify and was afraid to ask about. The next day, we toured Berwick Castle and Lindisfarne Monastery. This was a treasured place as the monastery was founded by St. Aiden, the first missionary to bring Christianity to England.

The following day, we took the train up to Edinburgh, Scotland. As soon as we walked out of the station, bagpipe music filled the air. The stonework of the buildings in Scotland was distinctively darker than in England. It was a foggy, rainy day, but it didn't stop us from enjoying our tour of Edinburgh Castle. We found it more impressive than the Tower of London, and the entrance fee was half the price. At the end of the day, we took our last train ride up to Glasgow where we would catch our plane in the morning. We stayed at another bed and breakfast in a little town called Lochwinnoch, just outside of the city. It had a beautiful garden where we relaxed and reflected on our memorable journey. By now we were a little weary from travel and ready to get home to our children.

The girls had a wonderful time with Pam and Mike's family. I was a little sad when I heard Bria accidentally call Pam "Mama" upon my return, but little Bri quickly assured me she indeed knew who I was. We spent a few more days all together enjoying each other's sweet company in Chicago before the long drive back to Albany. Once again, the kindness of friends and the faithfulness of God had made the impossible possible.

CHAPTER TWENTY-TWO

STAYING THE COURSE

The long-term goals you set as a family provide your marriage with a sense of purpose. Once the initial honeymoon phase is over, you need something greater than marriage itself to propel you forward as a couple. You need to revisit your family mission statement and regularly communicate the ways you're making progress toward your goals. Your common mission will help keep you connected, even when the steps toward those objectives are costly.

During our seventh year of marriage, Erv was finally able to see the light at the end of the Ph.D. tunnel. He had passed all of his qualifying exams, finished his coursework, and was wrapping up his dissertation research. He began applying for positions at Christian colleges to teach business. His very first interview was at a Baptist college in the Midwest. I was not excited about moving so far away, but Erv was determined to teach at a faith-based institution. He wanted the liberty to include biblical principles in his teaching. This choice meant we were definitely leaving Albany, a truth that did not sit well with me. We had lived in Albany for five years now, and it had become our home. We had a wonderful church, close friends, and family nearby. We were established and comfortable. But Erv had worked hard earning his degree, and I did not want my comfort to stand in the way of his dreams. I emotionally prepared for our family to move.

Erv was not offered the job in the Midwest, and I felt a sense of relief. I knew it was only a matter of time, but for now I celebrated our temporary stability. The girls were growing quickly, and both of them finally graduated out of diapers. It was a monumental event, five years in the making! We were enjoying Mikayla and Brianna immensely, and they blessed us with their smiles and funny antics every day. The four of us were relaxing with some friends on the front porch when we heard some very sad news. One of the families in our youth group had lost their oldest son. He had been struck by a car while crossing the road and did not survive. It was a tragic loss, and their youngest son was left an only child.

We couldn't help but wonder how difficult it would be for the younger brother to be left all alone after years of companionship. It made us consider our girls. They were very close and did everything together. We couldn't imagine if something happened to one of them, especially once they were teenagers. The loss to us as parents would be great, but we imagined it would be even greater for one of them to be left all alone.

When we were first married, we had wanted a family of at least three or four children. When the girls came so quickly and close together, we put the idea of a large family on hold. Was now the time to have another child? We had never planned a pregnancy before so this felt unusual. We gave the idea of having a third child some serious thought for about five minutes. That's all it took. I was instantly pregnant.

Erv continued to look for teaching positions throughout the school year. I cringed as he sent applications all across America. I really did not want to be a plane ride away from family, especially now that we were having another baby. I wanted this child to know his or her extended family. Annual visits at Christmas or summer vacation would not be sufficient. Everyone was so excited about this expected child. Some hoped it would be a boy and yet most assumed we would have another girl (we were good at making those).

The girls were very excited about their sibling-to-be. My growing belly was regularly rubbed and poked and hugged. Mikayla and Brianna attended sibling classes at the local hospital, learning how to properly hold, change, and feed the arriving baby. Erv's father was very attached to the girls and looked forward to our newest addition. "You're going to miss Carrie and the girls and the new baby when you move," he would tell Erv, "because I'm not letting them leave. They're staying here with me." I was tempted to take him up on this offer.

Fear is a terrible motivator. Fear is also an enemy of marriage. Fear causes us to dig in our heels and close ourselves off to possibilities. Fear makes us stubborn and unwilling to consider other options. My fear was limiting my ability to fully support Erv as he pursued his new career. Fear robs us of joy and therefore steals life from our marriage. I would not let fear win.

Be sure to keep fear at bay in your marriage. When you find yourself fearful, ask yourself, "Why? What is it that's causing me to be afraid?" Speak these fears out loud to your spouse. Be honest, but also give them the opportunity to address your fears. Listen with an open mind and trust their best intentions. When you trust your spouse, they act in a trustworthy way.

Erv was not trying to take me away from our support system but rather he was trying to provide for our family in a career he found meaningful and rewarding. I had promised to love and support him as long as we both lived. Moving to a new town could be the next great adventure for our marriage. Yes, there would be unknowns, but we would face these unknowns together. This was an opportunity to grow closer together as a couple and as a family. Instead of being fearful, I chose to embrace whatever came next.

Soon we learned of a teaching position just a few hours away at Roberts Wesleyan College. This was the opportunity we were waiting for. We could still visit family, and they in turn could visit us. We would be able to stay in touch with our friends and church family as well. I didn't know much about the school or the community, but this job became my first choice. My roommate from college had a friend who went to school there in 1991 and she really liked it. Oddly enough, her name was Carrie. If that Carrie liked it, surely I would too.

The upcoming year flew by as we prepared for several transitions. Because we were definitely moving at some point, I needed to make plans for the Campus Ambassadors ministry at the University of Albany. I was so excited when my friend Kim accepted the invitation to move to Albany. She would spend the year training with me and then would take over the ministry, providing a smooth transition from my leadership to hers when I moved. She would also provide me with a maternity leave (something I didn't bother to take after having Brianna).

We loved working together and enjoyed collaborating on plans and ideas for the school year. We had a common vision for campus ministry and often said that we "shared a brain" making us able to anticipate one another's thoughts. Kim moved into one of the downstairs apartments at our house and became an integral part of our family. She helped me care for the girls and was a weekly guest at our dinner table. Kim also joined us in our excitement about the new baby.

My pregnancy rapidly progressed and my belly grew to an enormous size. Apparently, my body easily returned to its stretched out state the third time around. Kim commented that I was, "as big as a house," and my own mother called me a "cow." (Before you take offense at my mom, you should know she was only responding to me saying I felt like a cow but it still felt weird to hear her call me one!)

When my contractions started, I called my mom. As tradition would have it, she immediately came to town. Due to a decrease in her health, she was no longer driving, but received a ride from a friend (a generous offer since she still lived two hours away). She could only stay the night, so we hoped the baby wouldn't be as slow to arrive as the girls had been. We took the girls to Erv's brother's house and headed to the hospital with Mom. Four hours later, they sent us back home. I wasn't making any progress. They said it must be false labor. This was embarrassing. I had been in labor twice before, surely I knew what it felt like. Apparently, I didn't. By the next day, I still wasn't in labor. Mom had to leave town with her friend and without a new grandbaby.

A week later, the contractions came back. Mom decided she would wait a while before coming to town this time around. It wasn't easy for her to get a ride, and she didn't want to take any chances. It's a good thing she didn't. I was sent home from the hospital a second time. Now this was really embarrassing. You would think it was my very first trip to the maternity ward. How could I get it wrong, again? I was officially a delivery room reject.

I went home embarrassed and disappointed. The contractions continued for a week! They would increase in frequency and intensity (meaning pain!), and then slowly decrease. They never disappeared altogether. As soon as I started to relax, they would increase again. It became difficult to sleep. It became difficult to work. It became difficult to move. I was tempted over and over again to go back to the hospital, but I was determined to wait until I was absolutely sure I was really, truly, without a doubt, in labor.

The day before our third child was due, my contractions started to increase in intensity, for the 400th time. They started coming faster and faster, but I would not go to the hospital. I would not be sent home a third time. They got closer and closer together, and Erv started to worry. He brought the girls to his brother's house, just in case. I still would not go to the hospital. "The next time I go to the hospital, I'm not leaving without a baby," I insisted. Erv headed to the car (which was full of gas, by the way). I stayed on the couch. What if I was wrong and I wasn't really in labor? I had to be sure. Erv honked the horn. I tried to stand up and ended up on the floor. I was in a lot of pain. I didn't know if I could walk. "I think I'm really in labor," I said to absolutely no one.

When we arrived at the delivery room, I was thrilled to hear the doctor announce I was truly and genuinely in labor. This time, I would not be leaving the hospital without a baby! When we came to the hospital on "failed attempt #1," we had been given the same delivery room where both Mikayla and Brianna had been born. It was very exciting to imagine all three of my children would be born in the exact same place. After "failed attempt #1," they wouldn't even give me a delivery room for "failed attempt #2." They simply stuck me in an observation room so I wouldn't waste anyone's time. Maybe I had been labeled a "faker." When they saw me come in the door for "attempt #3" unable to even walk, they offered me a delivery room right away. I asked for the very special "Mikayla and Brianna were both born here" room, but someone else was using my room! Instead of the large, pale green room at the end of the hall, we were given a small Pepto-Bismol pink room near the nurses' station. They probably wanted to keep a close eye on "Faker Starr."

This was funny to us because our ultrasound indicated that this child was likely a boy. Of course, we didn't totally believe them after the "don't paint" experience with Brianna's ultrasound, but we were hopeful to be adding a boy to the Starr family. Being born in a bright pink room wouldn't be the most masculine entrance into the world, however, we managed to pass the time in a fairly guy-honoring way. It was game one of the World Series—the Subway Series—Yankees v. Mets. With Erv a Mets fan and me a Yankees fan, it was an interesting dynamic. We had the game on in our delivery room, and we caught glimpses of the action between contractions. Because I was the one actually giving birth, the medical staff all sided with me. The Yankees came out on top, and our little boy came out right on time—our only child to be born on their due date. To this day, our son Connor is obsessed with being prompt.

Erv, baby Connor, and I spent the night in a private room on the maternity ward. We decided it was worth spending a little extra for a private room since I would be going home to mother three small children soon enough. I wanted to rest while I could. First thing in the morning, the big sisters came to visit their baby brother. Mikayla and Brianna climbed up onto the hospital bed with Connor and me, admiring their long awaited sibling. He was hugged and kissed and held and almost squished to death. They were instantly in love with this handsome prince.

Two days later, we all brought Connor home from the hospital. We weren't home five minutes when the phone rang. It was the Chair of the Business Department at Roberts Wesleyan College. He wanted to schedule Erv for an interview. This was an even better baby gift than the air conditioner I received the day I came home with Brianna!

ERV'S TAKE

There is a reality in our culture that is not true in many other parts of the world: family is less influential in our lives. We don't have parents help pick our spouse. We would abhor having to move in with our in-laws. Careers can move us far away, even when similar positions might be available in nearby communities. There are some healthy outcomes to this reality: we build new friendships and escape unhealthy patterns that define our families. We lose out as well, however, often missing out on cross-generational connections. We miss the support family can bring to the challenges and changes of life. For many, we end up with more isolated lives. This was the big cost of moving, even just hours down the road. Years later, it is still the hardest loss and sacrifice.

CHAPTER TWENTY-THREE

WHY LIVE ON LESS WHEN YOU DON'T HAVE TO?

After years of making sacrifices and living differently than everyone else, it was weird to finally be faced with the option of a normal life. Did we really want to be a typical suburban family? Did we want to work traditional jobs and live in a traditional house and send our children to a traditional school? These were options we weren't really faced with before. With a great job opportunity on the horizon, many new possibilities opened to us. It was an exciting time, but also a defining time in our marriage. Who we were and what we stood for was about to be tested.

Erv and I took a road trip to Rochester with baby Connor. While Erv was interviewing, I traveled around to the different college campuses in the area seeking a place to start a new Campus Ambassadors ministry if we were to move there. It was the first weekend of December, and all the little towns were decorated for Christmas. The different communities looked inviting, and the College at Brockport struck me as the perfect place to start a new ministry. We enjoyed meeting the Chair of the Division of Business and his wife, as well as the other faculty and staff at the college, and easily pictured ourselves living in this new community. We drove home hopeful this place would become our future.

A few days later, Erv was offered the job! We started to make moving plans. Now that I had seen where we were headed, I was no longer worried but excited about this next chapter of our lives. The timing could not be more perfect as the two bedroom apartment that seemed so large when we first moved in now seemed small and crowded. The girls had grown out of their cribs into bunk beds, and Connor was sleeping in a cradle in our bedroom. The small apartment was not made for a family of five. The postage stamp backyard had no room to run, and our street was too busy for Mikayla to learn to ride a bike. I was thrilled to start looking on the Internet for our new home!

I wanted to live in a house. A real house, not an apartment. I found a beautiful house for sale right across from the campus. It had four bedrooms, two bathrooms, a lovely front porch, and a yard with a pool. It was perfect. Erv, however, found something else. It was also near campus, had four bedrooms, two bathrooms, and a yard. But this house had something more. Something causing him to be giddy with excitement. It had a two car, attached garage with an apartment above it. An apartment we could rent out to help pay for our new mortgage. After collecting rent for four years, Erv was committed to multi-family housing. I was open to the idea, although I liked my house option a lot better than his. Unfortunately, both houses went off the market before we could even talk to a realtor. Again, our timing was terrible.

Two months later, we made a trip to Rochester for the weekend to meet with a realtor and look at houses in person. We were shocked at the mortgage we qualified for with Erv's new salary. This dollar amount was higher than we expected and made us face yet another temptation. If we bought a house at the maximum amount we qualified for, the high mortgage payments would make us feel constantly strapped for money. We had been strapped for money for years. We had worked hard so we didn't have to be tight on cash all the time. Why would we put ourselves back in the same position just to have a bigger house than we really needed?

This is a common temptation for many young couples. Mortgage companies will pre-qualify you for the maximum amount you are able to pay. Real estate agents show you houses in the upper limit of your price range and you are suddenly not satisfied with a cheaper, more modest house. You can technically afford a nicer home, but it takes all of your disposable income. This puts incredible pressure on your relationship. When money is tight, there is more tension in your marriage. In some circumstances, this cannot be avoided. When it comes to home ownership, however, you always have options. Choosing a modest home you can easily afford is more desirable than your dream home with nightmare mortgage payments.

ERV'S TAKE

Often the person selling you something can't look beyond the moment. They know if you walk away, the chance of you returning to buy is low. They know that if you purchase a house, you are not likely to be back in the near future to buy another. Forward thinking sales people realize that eventually you will be back for a second time and/or speak to friends and family about your experience, and thus see their role as serving your needs.

In the end, you own your financial decisions. You determine what is valuable and important. You make these choices visible each time you choose what to do with your money. Steward it well. As with your time, there will only be so much money that comes through your hands.

I will tell you that the choice to live in a multi-unit home has been a rich blessing for our family. The people who have shared our lives and homes have been like family. The added income has enabled us to experience things we never would have been able to otherwise. Maybe this means of earning more money is not right for you, but don't make that decision just based on what "everyone" else is doing. Remember, you only go where others don't if you do what others won't.

We found a beautiful, old colonial house just a few miles from campus we both fell in love with. It had four bedrooms and two bathrooms (our minimum requirements), but it also had a swimming pool, a beautiful front porch, a gorgeous fireplace, and most uniquely, land that backed up to a creek where we could go canoeing. It was a real temptation. Erv's mom and stepfather had given us a canoe for Christmas, and unfortunately, it didn't get much use. Strapping it to the top of our van and driving it somewhere after loading up three kids rarely happened. If we bought this house, we could leave our canoe by the creek side and use it whenever we wanted to! The house was available for private sale, so we made the family a verbal offer, taking $10,000 off their asking price.

Once the offer was made, Erv couldn't sleep. This house was at least $20,000 more than he planned on paying or could pay for comfortably. Even though it was technically less than we could afford according to the mortgage company, the monthly payments would mean squeezing every other area of our budget. There would be no wiggle room, and that made us both uncomfortable. We were sick to our stomachs and cancelled the deal two days later. Back at our apartment, we were disappointed. Our house-hunting trip to Rochester had been a waste, and we were right back where we had started. Discouraged, we tried looking on the Internet again. Erv could not believe his eyes. The original house he had chosen months earlier was back on the market—and with a reduced price!

We headed to Rochester for another round of house hunting, this time with all three children in tow. By now we had seen lots of homes with fireplaces, dishwashers, and large yards. They had generous square footage and charming features. We couldn't bring ourselves to pay for any of them. They just didn't seem to be worth the money. Surely we could find what we wanted for a more reasonable price. It was already May, and we were hoping to move at the end of June. We needed to find something this time around. It was on this third fateful trip when we met our ultimate temptation.

Our realtor showed us yet another beautiful colonial with a

front porch, large bedrooms, fireplace, and a brand new $30,000 kitchen. It was stunningly, amazingly gorgeous! I love kitchens. It's where I spend the majority of my time at home. The brand new cherry cupboards went up all the way up to the ceiling. The granite counters glistened in the sunlight as we made our way across the ceramic tile floor. There was a charming desk/work station right there in the kitchen. It would allow me to keep up with my ministry email and paperwork while making dinner and entertaining children. There was a breakfast bar where the three kids could enjoy an after-school snack while they did their homework. I could picture our whole family enjoying this kitchen. It only had three bedrooms, but with the kitchen desk, I wouldn't need an office. The girls could keep sharing a room, and it would be fine. We wanted that kitchen.

Before we could make any final decisions we needed to visit Erv's Internet find with the apartment over the garage. It wasn't available to show until the afternoon. I was fixated on the kitchen at the other house. Visiting this garage apartment house was simply a formality. Erv felt like it was not a coincidence when his house, complete with rental income, had come back on the market. He would not make an offer on the amazing kitchen house until he saw the garage apartment house. Brianna and baby Connor fell asleep in the realtor's car on the way across town, and I decided to let them stay in the car and rest while we looked at the house. Everyone wanted the amazing kitchen house, so they didn't really need to see this one. I expected us to be back in the car shortly.

We rang the doorbell of the white, Cape Cod style house. We entered the brown paneled breezeway and walked through the small, carpeted kitchen. The homeowner offered five-year-old Mikayla some Doritos, which she happily ate sitting at the kitchen table. Meanwhile, Erv and I investigated the rest of the house. It, indeed, didn't take long. There were two small bedrooms and a bathroom on the first floor, and a decent sized living room with a large picture window. Upstairs were two large bedrooms with lots of shelves and closet space as well as another full bathroom. I was intrigued. This house had much more space than it looked like from the outside. Then the realtor took us to the greatly anticipated garage apartment. It had a large, open kitchen, dining, living combination room, a separate bedroom, and a full bathroom. It was clean and bright and surprisingly spacious.

The realtor took us outside. There was a large back yard with a row of tall pine trees along the back, giving the illusion of being in the woods instead of suburbia. Then we were brought to another back yard, behind the pine trees. This house came with a double lot. From this yard, you could see the Roberts' campus. The realtor pointed out a brick building about 100 feet away. It was Carpenter Hall, the home of Erv's future office. This caught our attention. Walking to work would mean we could go back to one car and cut our automobile budget almost in half. This house became more and more interesting to us both.

This house didn't have a $30,000 kitchen, a fireplace, or even a dishwasher. The other house had all of the above. We were torn. Did we go with the economical choice as we had for the past seven years of our marriage—the smaller house with rental income and the walking-to-work, one-car option? Or did we enjoy Erv's new income and buy the beautiful house with the brand new kitchen of our dreams? We decided to make an offer on the amazing kitchen house. We had worked hard. Erv finally had a real income. We deserved a $30,000 kitchen.

Once the offer was made, we both felt sick. It was too expensive. We didn't need a $30,000 kitchen. We had made the same mistake again. It was not a wise choice. We should have chosen the smaller house with the rental income and the option to walk to work. We had allowed our emotions to cloud our better judgment. We tried to stay excited about our beautiful new kitchen, but we both knew it wasn't worth the cost.

Even though this was sad and frustrating, I was honestly glad we were on the same page. At least we were miserable together. When you share the same values, even your mistakes are an opportunity to grow together. We commiserated with one another instead of arguing. We attempted to comfort and cheer one another instead of blaming each other for our mistakes. We would stand united in this decision and support one another as we dealt with the consequences of yet another misstep.

Fortunately, our offer at the amazing kitchen house was rejected by the seller. They wanted more money. They were hoping we would counter with a higher price, but we didn't. We both breathed a sigh of relief and asked our realtor to write an offer for the garage apartment house. It was $20,000 less than the other house, and this home provided income from the apartment. Erv asked his dad if he would help put in a fireplace and asked his stepfather if he would help put in a dishwasher. Both said yes and our economical dream home was born!

CHAPTER TWENTY-FOUR

FAMILY FRIENDLY ADVENTURES

Each new home you live in is a fresh start. Whether you are switching apartments or buying a house, a new beginning is an opportunity to re-establish your priorities. Make plans for your new place together as a couple. Talk about what you want life to look like there. What needs to change about the way you are relating to one another at home? Where has your life together gone off track from your goals? Embrace the chance to realign your living space with your desired lifestyle.

One area where our marriage had gone off track was personal privacy. With five people living in a two-bedroom apartment, we rarely had time alone. We all shared one bathroom and were frequently interrupted by little girls who had to go pee, "RIGHT NOW!" The two girls already shared a bedroom so Connor had been sleeping in our room since he was born. We were determined to avoid this with both girls, but with limited space, we needed a quiet place for the baby to sleep. Even though he was just a baby, sex in a room with a sleeping baby is a little awkward. Our physical intimacy was suffering in our cramped little apartment.

In our new home, we moved all three kids upstairs and we stayed downstairs. While this may concern some parents, we believed our children were perfectly safe and our room remained perfectly private. The kids also had their own bathroom allowing us a little more privacy there as well. Since we're big believers in showering together, this meant fewer interruptions when we were conserving water.

Even in our old home, our children were so accustomed to us showering at the same time they were shocked to discover other families who didn't consider this normal. I remember visiting some friends of ours out of town for the weekend. The wife was in the shower and the husband was waiting for a turn. The husband was joking with our children, asking them if their dad was often stuck waiting for their mom to finish showering. Mikayla looked at him strangely and said, "No. Mom and Dad shower together. You should just go in there now!"

This same topic came up in phone conversations as well. Someone would call and ask, "Is your father available?"

"No," one of our sweet children would reply. "He's in the shower."

"Oh," the uncomfortable caller would say, "well, is your mother available?"

"Nope. She's in the shower too."

"Oh," the caller would say, now even more uncomfortable, "I'll try again later."

When we emerged from the bathroom, we'd have this conversation repeated back to us verbatim. After the incident repeated itself a few times, we trained our children to not answer the phone when we were in the shower. Other than these awkward moments, showering together is a great benefit to your marriage. It was one of the many advantages we appreciated about our new home, especially now that we weren't being interrupted by emergency visits from potty-trained kids.

We spent the very first night at the new house lighting sparklers on the front porch steps. Nine-month-old Connor sat in my lap as he held the bright, shiny sparkler, his hand wrapped securely inside mine. Brianna had just turned four years old and happily ran circles around the Mountain Ash tree in our new front yard. Five-year-old Mikayla chased behind her, laughing with joy.

Mikayla was probably the most excited about our new home. When we first arrived at the house, she charged through the door with a disposable camera in her hand. She ran into every room taking pictures. She snapped photos of every window, every door, and inside every closet. "This place is a mansion!" she exclaimed. "I never thought we'd live in a mansion!" Kids have the best perspective.

Erv's younger brother, Jason, and his wife, Heather, made the journey to Rochester and helped us get settled into our new home. Saying goodbye to them was the hardest part of our move. Erv's brother had lived in the apartment downstairs from us for two years. Once Jason married Heather, my childhood best friend, they moved into an apartment just a few blocks away. Heather had cared for our children during Campus Ambassadors meetings every week for five years while we were in Albany. She and Jason were always willing to watch the children and were the primary reason we never paid for a babysitter. They were disappointed about our move. They even considered looking for jobs in Rochester so they could live near us. We all cried as we watched their car head back to Albany the next day. This was going to be more difficult than I thought.

Our first few weeks in Rochester were quiet and surprisingly peaceful. It was strange to have days go by without the phone ringing. We felt a little bit like we were on a vacation. Living in this new home didn't seem like reality. The house felt mammoth (all 1,500 square feet of it!) after being squished in a two-bedroom apartment. The girls happily shared the large upstairs bedroom. For the first time, we had space to put both of their beds right on the floor. After years of bunk beds, this was a novel idea. There was also plenty of space for dance parties and fashion shows.

Connor had his own spacious room, also, right across the hall from his sisters. Erv and I were happy to have a bedroom to ourselves once again. It was about time for our little roommate to move out. Three expansive yards (almost a full acre of land) and a quiet neighborhood where the kids could safely play were a delight. All of the scrimping and saving so we could one day buy this house felt so worthwhile.

I woke up early each morning with Connor and roller bladed around our new neighborhood, pushing him in the stroller. He squealed and laughed as we spun around the corners. This was our special time together and an energizing way to start the day. My new neighbors grew to know me as the "rollerblading baby lady." Once we returned home, everyone was awake, and we'd plan the day's adventures.

We found many free or inexpensive outings for families around Rochester, including several beautiful parks and playgrounds and a free beach along Lake Ontario with concerts open to the public every Wednesday night. We signed the girls up for discount swim lessons at Roberts and purchased an annual membership to the local children's museum. For the same cost as two family visits without membership, we could go to this wonderful museum as often as we'd like all year long. Our family went at least once a month, making it well worth the investment. We purchased a membership to the city zoo with the same philosophy. The zoo has a fantastic stream where the kids could cool off by playing in the water between excursions to various animal habitats. In the summer, we visited the museum and the zoo almost weekly, earning our money back in the first month.

ERV'S TAKE

Kids are a delightful addition to your family. Embrace them into the culture you have already developed. Help them to learn to enjoy the things you enjoy. When they are older they may have similar or different interests than you. Either way, they will appreciate what is important to you and cherish the memories together.

My personal experience has been that young children do not cost a lot. There are some added costs, but tax breaks and family support can limit the cost of young children. This is less true if you have two working parents and need to pay for childcare. Young children are content with what we can provide, it is only later that they begin to learn discontentment from us. Their needs and wants grow and, similar to us, they long for things that they do not have. What we are teaching ourselves about contentment needs to be passed on to the next generation.

While enjoying lots of family fun, we also started working to transform our new house into our dream home. The house had two front doors—both bright pink. I hate pink. It is my least favorite color in the world. I have changed my favorite color about seven times in my life, and it has never, ever been pink. No house of mine was going to have pink doors. Not a chance. I purchased a quart-sized can of colonial blue paint (my current favorite color), and the pink doors were gone by day two of our residency.

As if pink doors weren't hideous enough, there was also carpet in our new kitchen. Who puts carpet in a kitchen? I could not understand it. When you have three small children, food gets spilled in the kitchen a lot. It's basically a daily occurrence. Cleaning sticky food off a carpeted kitchen floor is a completely unpleasant experience. I know because the girls spilled an entire jar of raspberry jelly on it day one. But carpeting in the kitchen had forced this home to be sold at a bargain price, so I didn't complain. I ripped it out. Of course Erv and his handyman dad helped me. A lot. We took the carpet out of the kitchen and the breezeway entry.

Erv and his dad laid ceramic tile, found for $1 a square foot in the clearance room of the local home repair store. Because the tile was a discontinued line, there were limited quantities of each color available. There wasn't enough of any one color to cover the floor. Dad's solution was to buy two different colors and lay them in a checkerboard pattern. The finished product looked great—far better than carpet—for minimal cost with our own labor. We were already increasing the value of our home.

We also painted over the dark wood paneling of the breeze-way, installed a gas insert fireplace, and added a chair rail. What was once a dark, chilly entranceway had now become a cozy, inviting family room—my favorite room in the house.

After discovering the hardwood floors of the living room extended into the dining room, we pulled up that carpet, as well. This was much more difficult than the kitchen. The carpet had been glued right to the hard wood floor! We had to melt each square inch with an iron and scrape the carpet and glue off the wood with a putty knife. It took hours and lots of patience. We then hired one of the maintenance workers from the campus to refinish our hardwood floors. We tried to do most jobs ourselves, but we were tentative about this one. This wasn't what our new friend did professionally, but he had just finished the gym floor at the college. He was comfortable with the job and gave us a discount price. The newly refinished floors turned out beautiful-ly. The house was transforming, making it a more enjoyable place to live. We were so glad we didn't overpay for a house in perfect condition. It was much cheaper to transform our discount house into the home we wanted.

Erv's much appreciated garage apartment completely lived up to our expectations. While the moving truck was still in our driveway, two different young couples from the college came to our door. They both heard we had an apartment and wanted to rent it. We never even advertised and had our choice of tenants! We enjoyed getting to know the lovely young couple we selected and found it to be a pleasure sharing our living space with them.

We also appreciated the rental income contributing to our new mortgage payment.

For our first year in Rochester, we chose to retain ownership of our apartment house in Albany, as well. Our friend, Kim, lived in the house and collected the rent for us. The additional income allowed us to purchase our home with a 15-year mortgage. This meant higher monthly payments but much lower interest paid over the life of the loan. This mortgage was later refinanced to a ten-year mortgage at an even lower interest rate. Most people considered this impossible, but we had become accustomed to living on less and we didn't mind the higher mortgage payment allowing us to avoid 30 years of interest!

Continuing to live below our means was an intentional choice allowing us to pursue even greater adventures. By selecting a home we could afford, we opened doors to travel to new, exciting places outside our four walls.

CHAPTER TWENTY-FIVE

NOT THE TYPICAL EUROPEAN VACATION

Erv was enjoying his new full-time teaching position at Roberts Wesleyan College, and I found starting a new Campus Ambassadors ministry at Brockport rewarding. Mikayla began kindergarten at the local public school while Brianna and Connor continued tagging along with me at work. Erv walking to work was a real benefit as he came home for lunch every day, allowing him to connect with the kids and me. It also meant an inexpensive, homemade lunch. Mikayla's half-day program at school meant we could continue our free trips to the zoo, parks, and children's museum throughout the school year on my days off.

We officially celebrated Erv's graduation with his Ph.D. in December. Mikayla was not happy to ruin her perfect attendance record in kindergarten but missed a day of school to attend the ceremony. I found myself unexpectedly emotional as I sat in the bleachers. This degree was a formidable mountain to climb, and it had taken its toll on all of us. I was extremely proud of Erv and personally thankful to have survived. I would no longer hear Erv say, "I'm not here. I have homework to do," as he sat on the living room couch at night. Now when the kids went to bed at night, we would finally have time for each other. That is, until I decided I had plans of my own.

Campus Ambassadors requires their staff to receive a seminary education. I always agreed with this policy on a philosophical level. However, with five years of working part-time in ministry and full-time as a mother of preschoolers, it hadn't exactly fit into my schedule. I was regularly asking for extensions to postpone my seminary education. Now with Erv finally finished with school, it was my turn to be a graduate student. With Erv working at Roberts, I could attend Northeastern Seminary at the college for free. Classes were held one night a week, specifically designed for people juggling school with work and family. It was a perfect fit for me. I was just hoping it wouldn't be too hard on us.

Erv and I were blessed to meet many new students on our respective campuses. I was excited to begin my ministry by working with international students at Brockport. After enjoying the rich diversity at the University at Albany, I was glad to meet students from around the world at this new campus. Erv had a special affinity for international students as well, and connected with one in particular on his campus named Russell. Holding duel-citizenship in Canada and Hungary, Russell brought a rich perspective to the classroom. Erv and Russell began reading books together on economics (the focus of Erv's undergraduate degree) and met weekly on campus for a time of discussion and mentoring. By the second semester, Russell invited us to visit him in Hungary the following summer. He also wanted to introduce us to some missionaries using business concepts to provide jobs for the poor in Romania.

Erv thought the idea of learning more about business and missions work in Hungary and Romania sounded very exciting. When Erv suggested we go there with Russell, I was tentative. Actually, I was terrified. Russell was going to be with us for the first half of our trip, but we would spend the second half on our own. We didn't speak Hungarian or Romanian. I loved the idea of assisting missionaries and seeing new places, but this was a little scary to me. Most short-term mission trips I knew of were done with a group, not a couple who had never been to that country before. When God provided free childcare for us once again, I had no excuse.

For the three hundred and twenty-sixth time, I adjusted my perspective and fought fear in favor of our marriage. We were just beginning to feel settled in our Rochester home. We were falling into a routine, which was comfortable but not stimulating to our marriage. We were both energized by activities and relationships outside of our home, potentially pulling us apart. We needed another adventure for just the two of us. This trip would be a new challenge we could tackle together as a couple.

Erv did some research online and found a great price on tickets. Russell used his hometown connections and missionary contacts to find us inexpensive housing in both countries. We arrived in Budapest with our carry-on luggage in tow. It's a good thing we pack light because Russell gave us a tour of the city by foot. We dragged our rolling luggage across the cobblestone streets, alongside the Danube River, and up to the Parliament building.

ERV'S TAKE

Tourist locations can be very relaxing and enjoyable. You can also have an amazing adventure traveling with a local. You will see the country/city/area in a different light. You'll gain firsthand experience of what day-to-day life is like. Many of our trips have included some form of service. We end up with new friends, incredible memories, and a sense of purpose and meaning.

I've learned how gracious people can be, and been humbled by my inability to communicate the simplest of ideas in a foreign tongue. At the same time, I've seen the needs in the world and it has expanded my heart for others. I hope we can pass this love of people and places on to our children. It is a central part of our family identity.

After touring Heroes Square, we headed by train to Russell's home city of Gyor. The train was completely packed like a can of sardines. We had to sit on our luggage in the aisle. When we arrived in Gyor, we found a charming little town with a center square lined with cafes and shops—a common stop for German tourists. Russell took us to a small inn where we would spend our first few nights. We had a tiny little room with slanted ceilings. If you sat up quickly in bed, or tried to enjoy using the space in unique ways because you're in another country with just your spouse, you smacked your head on the low ceiling. We learned this from experience, more than once.

Russell returned home to spend the night with his dad, and Erv and I were left to fend for ourselves for dinner. After a long day traveling, I was starving. I am blessed with a crazy high metabolism, so I'm accustomed to eating about every two hours. It had been almost 20 hours, and I was desperate for food. We chose a small restaurant just a few blocks from the inn. We were nervous about ordering on our own without Russell to help us, but it turned out to be an entertaining adventure. We both pointed to something on the menu and anxiously waited for our selections to arrive. We found drinks to be the easiest to order in both Hungary and Romania. Fortunately, a Coke is "Coke" all over the world.

Our time in Hungary felt more like a honeymoon than a mission trip. We enjoyed strolling around the beautiful town, eating delicious food, and having long, uninterrupted conversations. Other than the awkwardly slanted ceilings directly over our bed, our private little hotel room was the perfect place for romantic encounters. And unique challenges in the bedroom only invite creative solutions.

This was exactly the trip we needed. The longer we were married, the more obvious it had become that marriage takes intentional work. Experiencing new places together gave us fresh conversation starters and infused our familiar relationship with new energy. Our second night, after Russell had gone home, Erv and I ate out at Café Mozart, a charming outdoor café complete with wrought iron tables and chairs with blue umbrellas and white tablecloths. I felt like I was a character in a movie. The prices for food in Hungary and Romania were incredible. Most of our meals on this trip were eaten out, and we paid an average of $4 each per meal. I would not have thought to travel to

Hungary for a romantic vacation, but we found it to be perfectly lovely and pleasantly priced.

Traveling to outside-the-box locations is a wonderful way to have a unique experience with a lower price tag. The best adventures are not always found in the most obvious places. I had never dreamed of traveling to Hungary. I was barely aware the country of Hungary existed. I didn't know Hungary was spelled differently than hungry. And I definitely didn't consider it a romantic, tourist destination. When you're planning your next getaway, seek out a spot off the beaten path. Stay in a hotel recommended by the locals and eat where they eat. You'll still have a fantastic experience and pay a fraction of the cost.

ERV'S TAKE

When you are younger or have more time to travel, you can also work on farms or in hostels to help cover the cost of exotic travel. We have been in poorer countries like Haiti, Romania, and Guatemala...and modest countries like Hungary, China, and India...and wealthier countries like France, Germany, Switzerland, and Japan. In each country, we have met amazing people, tried unique food, shared incredible memories, and seen spectacular works of art, architecture, and nature. We have served, explored, and worshipped with a wide variety of people. The world may be small, but all of it is still worth exploring.

On the fourth day of our trip, Russell brought us to the train station to see us off to Romania. I didn't want to leave. Not only was I disappointed to vacate this beautiful place, I was scared to leave Russell. He had been our guide thus far, speaking the language and showing us the way to go. Now we would need to navigate on our own and somehow communicate what we needed. I pushed back my fear and confidently stepped into our rail car. We spent all day on the train from Gyor to Arad, Romania. It was hot and smoky, and it seemed we would never arrive. When we finally pulled into the station, my anxiety returned.

We needed to find our way to the home of Russell's missionary friends. I'm still not quite sure how we got there, but we managed to find the house. I was very excited to meet these kind American women serving the Lord in Romania. Later in the evening, they brought us to meet another missionary friend named Lee. He was from England, and he had an intriguing ministry to street children. He was providing housing and jobs for teens without homes. The boys he worked with ran a variety of businesses. Some worked the farm where they all lived. They raised pigs and vegetables. Others sold bicycles made from closeout parts donated to the ministry. Still others ran a bridal shop where they rented out wedding gowns. Lee found all kinds of creative ways to employ young adults instead of seeing them live in the streets. He was very inspiring. After spending another day touring Lee's various businesses, we packed up our bags and got back on the train. It was another long ride from Arad to Sighisoara. The views were stunning as we arrived in the Transylvanian Mountains.

In Sighisoara, we met two more American missionaries, Dorothy and Elizabeth. Dorothy had lived in Romania for several years and owned her own home. We stayed with Dorothy in a little apartment on the top floor of her house. From our window, we could look out over the red clay tile roofs of the other houses in the city. We spent the next day playing with young children in the family center, a part of the ministry where they served food and provided educational activities for those in need.

The following day was the most challenging of our trip. We visited a hospital for abandoned children. We volunteered with our new missionary friends, holding babies and playing with toddlers who had no families to visit them. We were given nursing scrubs at the front desk in the hospital lobby and instructed to put them over our clothes. We were told we could take any of the babies out of their cribs to hold them as long as we had the scrubs on. Having a baby of my own at home, it was heartbreaking to see row after row of cribs full of babies, with not a single adult in sight. We passed three rooms full of babies and still hadn't seen anyone caring for these precious children. As we made our way from room to room, holding the babies, I had to resist the urge to sneak one or two home with me.

It's good to be reminded of the needs of others. It is so easy to focus on our own needs and wants. When we are focused inward, we have a flawed perspective. This inward focus is also detrimental to our marriage. Nothing shows us how selfish we are the way marriage does. Trying to live every day of our lives in tandem with another person requires us to die to self on a daily basis. When we become self-centered, it does great damage to our relationship. If we regularly find ways to serve others in greater need, it reminds us as individuals and as a couple to put the needs of others first. When we see others in need, it allows us to count our blessings, thanking God for the things we do have in our lives instead of the things we don't have.

The longer you're married, the easier it is to find fault with your spouse. You know them so well. You know all of their weaknesses and hang-ups. If you are not intentional about focusing on the good traits, you can become bitter and resentful about the bad ones. You can find yourself noticing other people, attractive people, who have more desirable characteristics. Instead, you need to be thankful for all of your spouse's positive qualities. You need to consider others who have broken lives, who envy your happiness. Your marriage is a treasure to be cherished and protected.

By experiencing brokenness together as a couple, we became incredibly grateful for the life we have. We also became more generous. We had always looked for ways to give and share our resources with others. So many people had given sacrificially to us over the years. We were glad we could give even more now in our new stage of life.

Our last day in Romania was my birthday. We visited yet another ministry for underprivileged teens. Dorothy was using a similar model to Lee, using small businesses to help fund the needs of children whose families could not afford to care for them. One of their businesses was giving guided tours of the Citadel. Erv and I took a tour of the beautiful city, admiring the architecture, and enjoying the folklore. At the end of our tour, we treated our young guide to dinner at a local restaurant. We were shocked to learn she had never eaten there before because it was too expensive. Our dinners were only $3 each. This was a real eye-opener for us about the reality of poverty around the world. An extremely cheap dinner out for us was an extravagance to this young lady.

In the evening, we took one last, long train ride to Bucharest. We exited the train at 1 a.m. As we made our way from the outdoor platform to the station, several men came up on both sides of us, seeming to want to carry our baggage. We had been told not to accept any such offers. We'd been warned of the high crime rates at the train station and tried our best to ignore their menacing insistence to help. I continued to fight fear, feeling incredibly vulnerable in the middle of the night. We searched for a legitimate taxi driver, complete with certification papers, and asked for a ride to the airport. We took turns sleeping uncomfortably in the airport, waiting for our morning flight to New York.

We arrived back home with a newfound appreciation for all that we had and a vision for helping ministries through business opportunities. This was the beginning of our passion for social entrepreneurship, using business to solve social problems instead of simply making a profit. Erv would soon put this model to work as he entered a new business partnership with his cousin, Chris. Together Erv and Chris bought a rent-to-own store. This business had been established as a means to make furniture and appliances available to the poor by providing low monthly payments. The problem with this model was the interest charged through the payment plans. The customers were paying three times what the item was worth by the time they owned it. Erv and his cousin phased out this old model and instead promoted a "90 days same as cash payment plan," still making the merchandise more accessible to the poor without taking them for granted with interest payments. They held workshops for their customers, providing personal finance advice, including the benefit of the "90 days same as cash" program.

Erv enjoyed partnering and teaching with his cousin in this business. Although the business was actually located back in the Albany area, where Chris lived, he made visits to the company and spoke frequently to Chris on the phone. This new venture allowed him to bring real life experience into the classroom. He felt good employing sound business principles and celebrated achieving his dream of having his own business. The added income allowed us to give more and support other ministries. It also allowed us to save more for future business opportunities, multiplying our efforts to help others. Our unique travel experience had opened our eyes to new needs and new opportunities. We were thankful our earlier choices had opened doors for us to partner in such meaningful work.

CHAPTER TWENTY-SIX

PREPARING FOR ALASKAN PARADISE

We always knew we wanted to do something extraordinary for our 10th anniversary. We had been saving toward it since our visit to England four years earlier. Every month, we were consistently putting away a little more money. We were finishing our second year in Rochester, and Erv had a new co-worker in the business department at Roberts. Marcia had come from the corporate world and brought with her a wealth of experience. She and her husband had enjoyed extensive travel, and she served as an excellent getaway consultant. Of all the adventures she and her husband experienced, her favorite was an Alaskan cruise. This was her strong recommendation.

Erv came home from work excited to share his idea for our big anniversary trip. I loved the idea of a cruise but had always imagined sunning myself on a pool deck, sipping a drink with an umbrella in it. The thought of bundling up with a wool blanket gazing at icebergs did not have the same appeal, but Erv was determined that this was the dream vacation we were looking for. A Caribbean cruise was common. An Alaskan cruise was extraordinary!

We headed to the computer to do a little research. After discovering an Alaskan cruise would allow us to take helicopter tours of glaciers, ride bikes in the Yukon, and mush sled dogs through the snow, I decided Marcia knew what she was talking about! Learning from our Adirondack camping trip, we made sure to read the fine print. Each of these excursions would cost extra, but we decided they were all "once in a lifetime" experiences. We carefully planned our itinerary according to the amount of money we had saved. We scheduled one special outing for each day we would be at port. The rest of the time, we would take advantage of the meals and entertainment included in the price on the ship.

When choosing our cabin, we employed our family philosophy of determining our minimum expectation and then upgrading it one level. We use this process for all kinds of decisions, from the brand of toothpaste we buy to the cars we purchase. If you always buy the cheapest item possible, you feel dissatisfied. By taking the minimum standard and choosing a version just one level higher, you have a higher satisfaction rate, yet you still pay less than if you had moved directly to the premium option. Sometimes the minimum plus one standard will bring you to the highest option, but most of the time, it will save you money and give you the quality you need at the same time.

ERV'S TAKE

I used this "one level upgrade" recently when I purchased a motorcycle. It was a little newer than I might otherwise have purchased, and I have loved the rides as a result. This principle is not always an option, but when it is, we've found ourselves feeling less regret (buyers remorse) than purchase something too "cheap" or too "costly". It's similar to the story of The Three Bears. Not too hot/cold, not too hard/soft, and not too cheap/costly, but just right!

We decided we minimally wanted an outside cabin so we could enjoy the view. We upgraded this one level and chose a room with a balcony. We avoided the temptation to upgrade to a suite, assuming that we wouldn't be using the room much anyway. After all the fun we had in our romantically tiny hotel room in Hungary, we knew we could enjoy ourselves without a ton of extra space. We expected the private balcony to be a pleasant treat when we wanted to be outdoors but away from the crowd.

After making all of the arrangements, I realized we had more work to do. Neither of us had ever been on a cruise before. As we began sharing our excitement with friends, I was asked an unexpected question: "What are you going to wear?"

"Warm clothes. It's Alaska."

"No, I mean to dinner?"

I didn't realize you had to get dressed up for dinner on a cruise. I had only seen the people on cruises in commercials wearing bikinis. I knew I wouldn't be wearing one of those, but I didn't know I would be wearing fancy dresses. I didn't own any fancy dresses. We are not the dress clothes type. Even though Erv wore a suit to work almost daily, I had never been to the dry cleaner. I use those special bags you can put in the dryer to clean a husband's suits. It's much cheaper. I, myself, didn't have much occasion for wearing dress clothes. I enjoyed being paid to wear jeans and T-shirts to work every day. This is a huge benefit to campus ministry.

I looked at my closet. I did have a growing collection of bridesmaid dresses. This seemed the perfect occasion to finally get my money's worth out of those. As I tried them on one by one, none of them seemed fit for a cruise—they distinctly looked like bridesmaids dresses. I was in trouble. I looked at the cruise itinerary. There were three nights I needed to be dressed up. We would be seated at a table with the same people every night. I could not wear the same dress three times. I would need THREE nice dresses. This was ridiculous.

I got in the van, loaded the kids into the built-in car seats, and drove to my favorite Salvation Army store. They had a whole section of dress clothes. Surely they had something cruise-worthy. I filled my cart with every dress in my size, regardless of the style or color. I lined up the kids outside of my dressing room and the fashion show began. "Ooooo Mommy! You look pretty," Brianna would respond to every one. Mikayla would quietly shake her head "no." Since Mikayla is the source of my best fashion advice, I would return to my dressing room and try again. On dress #13, I got my first Mikayla head nod. It was a navy blue, tank style dress—simple, elegant, $7 plus tax. Sold!

We moved on to the Goodwill store. Having exhausted all of my options at the Salvation Army, I needed more inventory. Carrie Cruise Wear Fashion Show, Take Two. Another cart full of fancy dresses and another dressing room. Another line-up of small Starr children prepared to make their mommy look fabulous. More "oohs and ahhs" from Brianna. More head shaking from Mikayla. By now, Connor needed to be bribed with food just to sit still. Fortunately, my bag was stocked with granola bars, buying me time to try six more dresses. On dress #8, I got another head nod. And applause from Brianna. Connor joined in on the applause, and I felt slightly conspicuous. While my children sat on the floor happily clapping, I stood wearing a floor length black dress with a slit up the side. It had an open back with skinny horizontal straps going across. Purchase number two. $12.

I was out of granola bars for bribing Connor and out of patience. While most women enjoy shopping, I find it a completely unpleasant process. I decided that two dresses would suffice. On one of the fancy dinner nights, we would skip the formal dining room and opt for the midnight all-you-can-eat chocolate buffet. The thought made me wish I hadn't bought any dresses at all. Well, now that I had spent almost 20 bucks, I was definitely wearing them.

Some people are not comfortable buying used clothing. I don't fully understand why. When you bring it home, you wash it. If it has stains or rips, don't buy it. I've found items at Salvation Army brand new with the tags still on! Not only does shopping at places like Salvation Army and Goodwill save your family money (and put less financial stress on your relationship), you are supporting a great cause. Your purchase is essentially a donation. What a wonderful win-win situation! You get to enjoy the thrill of having something "new" and the store has more income to help needy people in your community. Shopping never felt so good!

ERV'S TAKE

Keep in mind we don't recommend buying underwear this way. We often over-value the new. It is amazing how "new" things quickly feel "old." We encourage you to consider "used" in many walks of life (home, cars, clothes) as a way of not over-paying. New feels so good, but only for such a short time. Often it can lead you to feeling badly, and that really hurts.

Too many of us find our identity in our clothing and outward appearance. We need others to tell us we're attractive to feel worthwhile. If this is you, you're overlooking a valuable source of affirmation. Your spouse should be your greatest source of positive feedback. If sharing words of encouragement and praise is not comfortable or common for your spouse, share with them your need to hear this affirmation. One way we guard the fidelity of our marriage is to receive affirmation at home. As in all areas of marriage, it starts with you. Be sure you are affirming and encouraging to your spouse. Set the standard you would like to experience from them.

Before we left on our cruise, Erv's student, Russell (who, remember, was Canadian as well as Hungarian) gave us some friendly traveling advice. He encouraged us to fly into Seattle and take a bus into Vancouver. This would be much cheaper than flying directly into Canada. We drove the kids four hours to Albany where they would spend the next week with Aunt Heather and Uncle Jason. The next morning, Jason drove us to the airport before dawn. We felt like typical tourists checking luggage. I didn't want to squish my fancy new dresses into a carry on, and Erv felt his suits would survive better in a garment bag, as well. I also wanted to make sure I had plenty of layers for our outdoor excursions. When we arrived in Seattle, we checked in with the bus company. We had plenty of time to get to Vancouver before our cruise set sail. We boarded the bus, excited to be one step closer to our exciting journey.

We soon discovered something was wrong—very wrong. You know you're in trouble when your bus driver begins looking at a map while driving. He would pull into a parking lot and turn around. Then he would look at the map again. Then he would turn around again. Our confidence in him was waning. We studied our watches. We had less than two hours until our cruise was scheduled to leave. The two hours became one hour. One hour became 30 minutes. When we finally pulled up to the cruise terminal, it was empty. There was no one in line at the gate. We hurried up to the counter and presented our tickets. "Skip the check-in procedures. You need to go right to the dock. Your boat is about to launch!"

Erv and I took off running toward the boat. We sprinted down the dock, pulling our heavy luggage behind us. I was regretting the fancy dresses and warm layers. I should have stuck to our standard of carry-on luggage only. As our bags bounced behind us on the dock, the crew was preparing to pull up the gangway. We were the last passengers to board, and then the boat pulled away from land. That was more adventure than we bargained for.

CHAPTER TWENTY-SEVEN
EXTREME ADVENTURING

We love to explore. It's one of the hallmarks of our marriage. We're both curious people who love to learn and discover. From the moment we stepped on the ship, we were captivated. It was massive and not what either of us had expected. We definitely felt like a couple of kids in a gigantic candy shop. We wandered up and down every floor, mesmerized.

Our ship was a floating city with multiple restaurants, theatres, and shops. We eventually discovered our cabin during our extensive, self-guided tour. It was perfect. Every wall was covered with mirrors to make the small room appear larger. As a visual guy, Erv thought the mirrors were a serious bonus for this anniversary excursion. We spent a lot more time in our cabin than we originally thought we would. It turned out to be our favorite place on the ship.

The very first morning, we were sitting out on our little balcony reading when we spotted a killer whale jumping in the water below. The ship followed along the whale's path for several minutes before changing course. It was an incredible sight to behold! We were so glad we had spent a little extra on the balcony room. In one awesome moment, we considered the extra money well spent.

Each morning, we took advantage of the on-ship workout facilities. The treadmills faced toward enormous windows looking over the bow of the boat. As we ran, it felt like we were skimming across the water. Because all our meals were included, we indulged in three meals a day. Typically when we travel, we reduce our food costs by eating only two meals supplemented by snacks. We were enjoying three meals a day, plus snacks. It's a good thing we started each morning in the gym. The typical cruise passenger gains a pound a day on board. We could easily see why!

We were so excited about our first stop in the capital city of Juneau. This was our dog sledding day, and we both expected it to be our favorite. It was cloudy as we exited the ship, but it didn't dampen our spirits. We were going dog sledding in Alaska, one of the coolest things on earth that two people could do! We walked to the designated terminal and donned our glacier boots. We would travel by helicopter over the Mendenhall Glacier to the dog sled camp. This was going to be incredible. We were led to the helipad and climbed up into the chopper. Erv and I put on our headsets and gave each other a thumbs-up.

We waited to take off. We waited some more. Something was wrong. It started to rain. Then it started to pour. It was no longer safe to fly with the helicopter. Our tour was cancelled. We couldn't believe it. We exited the chopper and walked away dejected. We wandered aimlessly through the little tourist shops along the main street. It was totally and completely boring. We walked through the rain, disappointed at our luck. The highlight of our trip had become a dismal failure. We boarded the ship and pulled away from our favorite excursion opportunity. I was not excited to put on one of my new fancy dresses for dinner. We would comfort ourselves with all-you-can-eat ice cream instead.

Life is full of so many disappointments, great and small. One way to avoid pain is to lower your expectations. If we expect little, we are less upset when we don't get our way. While I do find it helpful to consider the worst case scenario, this is a depressing way to live all the time. Yet, when we have sky high hopes, we are setting ourselves up for failure and disappointment over and over again. You need to find a balance somewhere in between. There is no place where this is truer than in marriage.

We all enter marriage with expectations. We hope our partner will meet our needs and make us happy. We don't expect them to disappoint and hurt us. We certainly don't want to walk around every day anticipating pain from our spouse. This would make our relationship unbearable. And yet, when we expect our spouse to be superhuman, we will surely be disappointed when they are not.

When pain and disappointment come, whether it's directly from our spouse or simply shared with them, we have an option. We can melt down and allow it to ruin us, or we can rise above it. When dealt this disappointing blow on our anniversary cruise, it had the potential to ruin our entire trip. Yet love compels us to persevere through the pain. The disappointment was real and we allowed ourselves to feel it, yet we didn't stay in that negative place. We rallied our hopes and allowed ourselves to expect good things.

There were two more stops along our trip. The next port was Skagway. It was the only other town along our route that even offered dog sledding and helicopter tours. We had already reserved (and paid for) a narrow rail Yukon train/bike tour that would occupy four hours of our day. The Skagway dogsled tours were all sold out. Erv refused to give up hope. I love this about him! When we docked at 6 a.m., Erv was the first person off the ship. He knew the cruise ships worked in conjunction with local tour companies and decided to work with the tour company directly. I was still asleep in our cabin when Erv returned at 7 a.m. "It's raining and all of the morning helicopter tours are cancelled." This was not "good morning" news.

We went to the gym and breakfast, as usual, and disembarked for our train ride. At least this was not cancelled due to weather. We boarded the White Pass Yukon Route Railroad. The train ride through the majestic mountains was beautiful and the historic narration of the gold rush interesting. There was a small landing outdoors between each of the cars. I enjoyed standing out there, feeling the cool wind on my face. The air was so crisp and clean. It was still cloudy, but the rain had slowed to a light drizzle. There was only one dogsled tour in the afternoon, but helicopter tours were scheduled for every hour. Maybe there was hope we could take an afternoon helicopter ride. We tried to focus on the moment and take in the beauty around us. We chose to be thankful for what we could experience instead of what we couldn't.

When we reached Fraser, British Columbia, everyone taking the rail/bike tour exited the train. We were each given helmets and bright yellow windbreakers. The color was obnoxious, but it was good protection from the drizzle. Erv and I enjoyed speeding down the mountain on our borrowed bikes. Having been on several multi-day bike tours, we decided this was the way to handle big hills: take the train up and the bike down. We had crossed from Alaska into Canada while on the train up. On the way down, we got to bike across the border. It was fun to show our passports at the border patrol while on our bikes. The view along our ride was fantastic. We passed majestic waterfalls and steep mountain cliffs.

By the time we got back to town, the weather had cleared, and we learned the helicopter tours were now running. Unfortunately, the tour company told us every tour sold out while we were gone. We had missed our last chance to take a helicopter ride or a dog sled tour while in Alaska. Erv refused to take no for an answer. He left the tour office and set out on foot, heading straight out of town. I thought he was crazy. "I can see helicopters taking off and landing in the distance," he said. "The airport must be this way. We're going there!"

I reluctantly followed my husband. This reminded me of our trek to the Colorado River at the Grand Canyon on our honeymoon. Ten years later and I was experiencing the same exact scenario. Once Erv had his mind set on something, there was no changing it. We walked for miles, heading further and further away from our ship and all our free food. I was hungry. I tried to convince Erv to turn around. He ignored me. "You can go back if you want to. I'm riding a helicopter." Of course, I kept following. We were celebrating our 10th anniversary. I wasn't interested in hanging out on a cruise ship all by myself —even if they had incredible food in massive quantities.

Sure enough, Erv found the airport about four miles outside of town. We hadn't needed the morning workout after all since we power-walked the entire way chasing helicopters. Erv walked up to the ticket counter. "All of our helicopter tours are sold out," the attendant told Erv. "Told you so," was my immediate thought. "But I can put you both on stand-by. If someone doesn't show up, you can have their spot."

The dog sled camp was far up in the mountains. With the cloud cover, it was too dangerous to go, so the dog sled tour was cancelled. They were, however, still running helicopter glacier tours. I couldn't believe it. The door of possibility was open. It was only open a teeny, tiny crack, but it was open. We had already walked all this way. We decided we might as well wait and see if we could get on a flight. I raided the vending machine for a much needed bag of Skittles and grabbed an outdated magazine to pass the time.

We had waited for more than an hour when our names were called. A passenger on the next flight was more than 250 lbs. and wasn't willing to pay for two seats. If we were willing to buy two tickets, we could board the next flight. Although it had already been an expensive day with the train/bike tour, we decided it was worth it. We had planned on spending this much in Juneau and had received a refund. It wasn't a hard decision to purchase those two helicopter sightseeing tour tickets. I was so glad I hadn't said, "I told you so!" out loud. I would have eaten more than just Skittles that day—I would have eaten my hasty words too.

We put on glacier boots and boarded the helicopter. We donned our headphones and felt a strange sense of déjà vu. This time, we waited until the helicopter actually took off before giving each other thumbs up. The ground dropped away beneath us, and there was a sudden feeling of weightlessness. We climbed our way into the sky, following along a mountain ledge. As we reached the top of the mountain, it felt strange to keep on flying. The sensation was so similar to being on a roller coaster. I expected to go plunging back down toward the earth. As we traveled along through the sky, we passed over several glaciers. The incredible blue coloring reminded me of Superman's secret palace. It looked surprisingly delicious.

Halfway through our tour, we actually landed right on one of the glaciers. The pilot let us out so we could walk around. We explored the glacier and its giant crevasses. I was so tempted to jump across these giant cracks in the icefall. Considering each crevasse was at least three feet wide and hundreds of feet deep, Erv did not approve of my plan. He dragged me away from the death cracks, and we spent half an hour trekking around the glacier before re-boarding the helicopter. We took off and headed back to the heliport, enjoying incredible views of more glaciers and mountain ranges along the way. We absolutely loved our experience and found it well worth the cost. As we exited the chopper, we commented on how surprisingly easy it was to get a flight on standby. While leaving the heliport, we overheard someone comment that the dog sled camp had re-opened!

We rushed to the ticket counter. Had we heard correctly? Was the dog sled camp indeed open? Could we catch a flight? "Sorry. The dog sled tours all booked up while you were gone. You can try waiting for standby if you'd like."

We waited. It had worked before. What were the chances of it working again? We at least had to try. This would be our ultimate Alaskan experience, and it was our very last chance to make it happen. We waited and waited. This time I bought some Reese's Peanut Butter Cups and grabbed yesterday's newspaper. Our patience and perseverance were tested, but we remained buoyed with hope.

We could not believe it when our names were called! There were two seats open on the last trip to the dog sled camp. The trip was very expensive. We had already spent more money on this day than we had buying our living room furniture. This single vacation day was going to end up costing more than our wedding day. We bought the tickets. It was a record spending day for the Starrs, but it had all been in cash we had diligently saved. We both agreed this collection of unique experiences was well worth the high cost.

We loved the second helicopter ride and decided we someday want to own a helicopter. It was such an incredible feeling. We reached the dog sled camp and met our team. We were introduced to each dog by name. We petted each one to greet them. They were so beautiful and friendly. We were given hats and gloves to ward off the extreme cold of the high mountains. After receiving instructions of how to command the dogs, we mounted our sleds. The wind whipped around us as the dogs pulled us across the frozen ground. Snow sprayed our faces. At first we went slowly, then we picked up speed. I couldn't believe how fast the dogs could go pulling us behind them.

Half-way through our ride, we stopped to give the team a rest. We both got off to pet each one and tell them what a great job they were doing. We took turns "mushing" on the way back to the camp. Fortunately, I was better at this than punting in England. Maybe I had found my calling and someday, Erv and I would be giving helicopter/dog sled tours in Alaska. Before leaving the dog sled camp, we visited with some adorable sled dog puppies. It was a delightful end to an expensive and wildly satisfying day.

We spent the next day at sea, sailing through Glacier Bay. The decks were crowded, and we were glad to enjoy the view from our private balcony. As we sat huddled under a red, plaid blanket, I remembered my vision of this cruise when Erv first presented the idea. This was exactly what I had imagined—and it was blissful. The water was a bright, bluish-green from the mineral deposits in the glacier. As we left the bay, we passed a brown bear and her cub on the shore—an incredible sight! In the evening, after dinner, we enjoyed a musical in the ship's theater. We had attended a different show every night, and we found them to be a delightful way to end each evening. We marveled at the incredible experiences we were having.

I was a little nervous about our actual anniversary. This was the only day we had selected an excursion that was not one of my top choices, but Erv was enthusiastically looking forward to it, and I didn't want to spoil his excitement. I would be a good sport and endure. I prepared myself to go snorkeling. Who goes snorkeling in Alaska? I am not a good swimmer. Erv assured me that the ¼ inch thick neoprene wetsuits would keep me afloat. I was concerned that they keep me warm. We neared the water's edge, and there were large chunks of ice floating in it. We had just passed massive glaciers in the water the day before. This seemed a ridiculous idea—which is exactly why Erv loved it.

We were part of a group of 20 people, and each was given gloves and hoods to wear to keep us warm in the water. Once we began swimming, it was impossible to tell one person from the next. Everyone's faces were covered by the hood, goggles, and snorkels except for a small area around our mouths. I had no idea where Erv was. There were three guys with visible facial hair in the group, so I nonchalantly tried to follow them around, hoping one of them was Erv. Usually I could identify Erv by his unique height, but in the water, all the heads were at the same level.

Once I got over my initial nervousness, I found my underwater exploration to be completely enjoyable. We saw beautiful jellyfish, sea urchins, salmon, and many other creatures I cannot name and will not try. I even managed to pick the correct facial-haired guy at one point and was able to snorkel hand in hand with Erv. While it wasn't the anniversary experience I would have imagined, it turned out to be a wonderful way to celebrate our ten years of adventure together. Once we were out of the water, warm and dry, we toured the charming shops of Creek Street in Ketchikan. Erv surprised me by purchasing a simple, but beautiful, sapphire and diamond ring to commemorate the occasion. I'm not sure which I enjoyed more, the new ring or the saleslady thinking we must have married in elementary school to be celebrating our 10th anniversary.

As we sailed back to Vancouver, Erv and I reflected on our trip. It was hard to imagine that ten years ago we started our journey together in a borrowed tent. Today we were standing on our private balcony on a cruise ship in Alaska watching dolphins play in the water below. We hadn't received an inheritance from a rich uncle. We hadn't won the lottery (neither of us had ever even purchased a ticket). We had simply made consistent choices to spend less than we made. We had stuck to our values, pursuing our shared mission together. We saved and invested in ourselves and in others. And now we were enjoying the precious reward of the adventure of a lifetime.

ERV'S TAKE

Money has three broad purposes: to buy things (we need or enjoy), to bless others (gifts and giving out of generosity), and to make more money (so we can do more of the other two). By itself, money is of little value. It holds no pleasure until it is released. So, save, give, and spend.

We are so thankful to share our lives with you through this book. Thank you for the gift of your time. May the wisdom in these pages bless you, and the ignorance not limit you. May God richly bless you and your marriage, from now until the end of your days.

ACKNOWLEDGMENTS

Excellent Editors: Sarah George and Rebekah Barringer

Amazing Marketers: Steve Carter, Stryker Ostafew, Chris Nagle, Terrell Brady, Taylor Isselhard, Aaron McGinnis

Cool Cover Design: David Messner, Ethic Media, The Wonder Grove

Super Secret Agent: Michael L. McGinnis

Incredible Indiegogo Backers:
John-Erik Moseler
Lashawn Boyd
Thea Nelson
Ben Arment
Rob Alcorn
Terrell Brady

Bob and Meg Hartman
Krista and Steve Bovee
Gina Parris
Chris Nagle
Victoria Urbanczyk
Peter Lagueras
Liz Thrush
Hayden Hoebeke
David Messner
Stryker Ostafew
Thomas Ried
Marilyn Ostafew
Alana Matteson
Aubree and Jon Cleek
Sara Hill
Priscilla Drew
Phillip Sennett
Clara Manak
Lisa Carter
Aubree Rider
Sean Pritzkau
Gina Iannucci
Jessica Aiduk
Michael McGinnis
Heather Starr
Stacy Goebel
Joel Ashcraft
Leah Free
Mark Jennings
Susan TerHaar

Colin Conaire

Angela Buikema

Katheryn O'Donnell

Elizabeth Trieber

Jillian Chilson-Pietruch

Brenton Riling

Amanda Shifflett

Aaron Callahan

Linda Altobelli

Ryan A. Miller

RJ Clarke

Justin M. Snyder

Sullivan Slentz

Damara Rodriquez

Joanne Costain

Jenna Kepich

Charlene Isselhard

Taylor Isselhard

Katy Martin

Thomas Boto

William Harris

Steve Carter

Erin Nichols

David and Sarah George

Tracy Williams

Dawn Lovejoy

Amber Pusatere

Scott Austin

Kathleen Mathewson

Christine Lendway

Beka Watts

Kathleen Raniewicz

Stephanie Rezsnyak

Amy Bartholomew

Oliver and Christa Cabrera

Jennifer Putthoff

Pat and Nancy Wilson

Michelle Cronk

Judy Buss

Amy Jacobs

Morgan Skiff

Kathryn Garrett

Joshua Thurston

Laura Cook

Rachel Anderson

Troy Olson

Stuart Wilkins

Kathy Mercer

Jennifer Mitolo

Lily Pyke

Rebekah Barringer

Georg Drees

CPSIA information can be obtained at www.ICGtesting.com
Printed in the USA
BVOW042349260313

316534BV00003B/8/P